Oscar B. Parkinson

Outlines of Commercial Law

What Business Colledges Have Been Looking for

Oscar B. Parkinson

Outlines of Commercial Law
What Business Colledges Have Been Looking for

ISBN/EAN: 9783337232313

Printed in Europe, USA, Canada, Australia, Japan

Cover: Foto ©Suzi / pixelio.de

More available books at **www.hansebooks.com**

Outlines of
Commercial Law

What
Business Colleges
Have Been
Looking For.

A California Work
by a California Lawyer

We Present This Book

to the consideration of the Commercial Colleges of California, with the feeling that it will fill a place heretofore unoccupied.

We call attention to the following points of advantage possessed by this work:

FIRST. It is prepared especially for use in California, and has the essentials of the law of California, regarding business transactions, embodied in it.

SECOND. It is prepared by a lawyer in active practice in the Courts of California, who has also had some nine years' experience as a teacher.

THIRD. The work contains more law, in less space, than general text books, published for use throughout the United States, in this: that it does not need to state generally what the law is, and then state "that there are numerous exceptions, and the student will have to look at the statutes of his own state in order to find out what the law is there."

FOURTH. The book is written in the concrete, rather than the abstract, and contains numerous illustrations.

FIFTH. The illustrations, so far as possible, are taken directly from reports of cases decided by the

Supreme Court of California, and of other states where the same law exists, so that the illustrations can be relied upon as stating the law correctly.

SIXTH. The book is not padded with an appendix of useless and misleading "forms." A number of the more common and necessary forms are given in the body of the work.

SEVENTH. The work does not deal with generalities, but states the exact law correctly regarding business transactions.

EIGHTH. It is so arranged as to be valuable as a reference book for students after finishing their College course; hence a College should have no second-hand volumes on hand, but can sell new books to each class.

NINTH. The book is up-to-date, and any amendments made to the substantive law, by future Legislatures, will be supplied gratis, in the form of supplements, thus keeping the work strictly up-to-date.

We respectfully invite correspondence in regard to the work, and solicit your orders.

For further information, address

O. B. PARKINSON,

Stockton, California.

OUTLINES OF COMMERCIAL LAW

OUTLINES

OF

COMMERCIAL LAW

A TEXT BOOK FOR SCHOOLS
AND COLLEGES

BY

O. B. PARKINSON, LL. B.

OF THE

STOCKTON, CALIFORNIA, BAR

STOCKTON, CAL.

1898

PREFACE.

The fact that most authors of Commercial Law text-books heretofore published have endeavored to supply a text-book which could be used in every State in the Union, and at the same time sufficiently condensed to be within the scope of a college text-book, and consequently have omitted many important details relating to the every-day business law of particular States, is the reason for the production of this work.

This book is based on the Codes and Statutes and judicial decisions of the State of California, and is designed for use on the Pacific Coast.

We have endeavored to avoid general statements, which are always misleading, and have tried to supply the exact law applicable to each subject treated.

We have refrained from any extended discussion of remedies or practise in Court, as they are matters which are understood only by regular attorneys of long practice, and can not possibly be elucidated in the few pages we might devote to them.

We have supplemented abstract statements of law with numerous examples showing their application, and would call especial attention to this feature, as well as to the test questions requiring thoughtful work on the part of the student.

Besides the Codes and Statutes referred to, a number of other works have been freely consulted.

The illustrations given, so far as possible, are taken from decided cases of the Supreme Courts of the various States, and of the United States, so that such cases can be relied upon as stating the law correctly.

We have omitted the usual collection of forms for the reason that a form seldom can be made to apply to the case at hand, and consequently serves rather to confuse than aid.

O. B. PARKINSON.

Stockton, Cal., November, 1898.

CONTENTS.

(vii)

viii   CONTENTS.

COMMERCIAL LAW.

CHAPTER I.

HISTORY AND INTRODUCTION.

Whenever and wherever in the history of the world there has been an association of persons, some rule or regulation of conduct has been found necessary.

The first law that we have any record of was almost coincident with the creation.

A prohibitory law was given to Adam and Eve in the garden of Eden, and a punishment was meted out for disobedience of that law; and through all authenticated history from that time to the present, there has been no country or nation able to maintain itself without some code of laws.

When the wants of people were few and easily supplied, few regulations were required for their government, but as education, arts, sciences, commerce, and civilization generally, have been gradually extended during the centuries, law has become not merely a collection of rules, but a distinct science, consisting of a most complex system of regulations calculated to define and specifically set forth every act and thing which a person may be called upon to do in his intercourse with his fellow-men.

While it is impossible to explain the meaning of law in a single definition, the following may be sufficiently accurate for the purpose of this work: "Law is a rule of action dictated by some supreme power capable of enforcing obedience or punishing disobedience."

Law generally may be classified as Natural, Moral, and Human, or Municipal. Municipal Law consists of those rules prescribed by the supreme power of a state or country, declaring what is right and proper, and forbidding what is wrong.

It is with Municipal Law that we have to do in this book, and only with that division of Municipal Law which is called Civil Law.

CRIMINAL LAW is that division of Municipal Law which prohibits acts which are against public peace and harmony, and provides penalties for the punishment of wrongdoers.

Such crimes as murder, robbery, and forgery, and the punishments of fine, imprisonment, and death, are included in the Criminal Law.

CIVIL LAW comprises the rules regulating the rights of individuals in their business relations with each other, and the remedies for the breach of such obligations; as in case A owes B $100, the law declares that B has the right to collect it, and in case A refuses to pay, the law provides a means for compelling payment.

SOURCES OF LAW.—The most ancient source of part of our modern law is the unwritten law established in England many years ago, and which has since been mostly written. It is called the Common Law.

The English emigrants brought with them the laws of England, so that this Common Law became transplanted throughout the United States as the English-speaking people gained control of this country.

STATUTE LAW consists of the enactments of the United States Congress and of the Legislature of the several states. In California most of the Statute laws are incorporated in volumes called Codes.

The Commercial Law is for the most part contained in the Civil Code and the Code of Civil Procedure.

CONSTITUTIONS AND COURTS.—The Constitutions of

the United States and the State Constitution, and the judicial decisions of the Supreme Court of the United States, and of the Supreme Court of each State, are further sources of law.

CONFLICT OF LAWS.—There being so many sources of law it is often the case that the law as declared from one of these sources conflicts with or is opposed to the law as declared from some other source, hence it is important that we should know which law will govern in case of a conflict.

The Constitution of the United States is highest in authority, and extends over all the states, and the states are allowed to make only such local laws as do not conflict with the Constitution of the United States.

The laws of Congress are next in order, and are in force in every part of the United States. The State Constitution comes next and has authority within the limits of the state. Next to the State Constitution are the Statutes passed by the State Legislature. Lastly, the Common Law regulates subjects upon which the other sources are silent. The laws of one state have no authority in and can not be enforced in any other state.

INTERNATIONAL LAW.—Each country has its own laws, and has no right whatever over the persons and property of another country; but for mutual protection, the leading nations of the globe have, by common consent, and by agreements and treaties, formed what is known as International Law, or the Law of Nations, which all nations are in honor bound, and in honor only, to respect; e. g., it would be a breach of International Law for a neutral nation to aid with ships or munitions of war one of two nations which are at war with each other, or to protect and refuse to deliver or punish pirates. There is no means of enforcing obedience to International Law except by war.

ADMIRALTY AND MARITIME LAW.—Admiralty Law consists of the rules of a nation regulating commerce and shipping on the high seas.

Admiralty jurisdiction extends to acts done on the high seas during a war, while Maritime jurisdiction extends to contracts touching rights and duties pertaining to commerce and navigation in time of peace.

Under these laws the term "High Seas" includes the Great Lakes and navigable rivers, even within the limits of a single state. The United States Courts alone have jurisdiction over cases between American citizens arising under these laws.

COMMERCIAL LAW.—The subjects which form the principal part of this book were originally a part of the Common Law, and are derived mainly from the customs of the merchants of London and Liverpool, and for that reason the particular part referring to negotiable paper and business transactions has been called the "Law Merchant."

The legal maxim, "Ignorance of the law excuses no one," applies in business transactions as well as where a criminal offense is committed. No one can say that he did not know what the law was, and thus escape the consequences of his acts, hence it is important that every one should have a practical knowledge of the laws of business.

TEST QUESTIONS.

1. Distinguish critically between Criminal Law and Civil Law.
2. Name the different sources of law in the order of their present authority.
3. The captain of a vessel on Lake Superior runs his vessel into and damages another vessel. Under what general law should the damage suit be brought?
4. What was the Law Merchant?

CHAPTER II.

CONTRACTS.

CONTRACTS are the basis of, or enter into, almost every transaction in business life, hence they naturally and properly should be studied first as a whole.

The different subjects treated of under the title "Commercial Law," such as agency, partnership, insurance, and negotiable paper, are merely branches of the Law of Contracts.

DEFINITION.—A Contract is an agreement for a consideration to do or not to do a certain thing.

The word "agreement" implies that there must be at least two persons as parties to the Contract. A mere voluntary promise upon the part of one individual without any corresponding promise on the part of another is not a Contract.

ESSENTIALS OF CONTRACTS.—It is essential to the existence of a Contract that there should be:

(1) Parties capable of contracting.

(2) Their consent. agreement.

(3) A lawful object.

(4) A sufficient consideration.

Each of these essentials will be fully considered in subsequent chapters.

Contracts may be either express or implied, written or oral.

An EXPRESS CONTRACT is one the terms of which are stated in words; as for example, A says to B, "I will sell you this horse for $50." B says: "I accept your offer. Here is $50." This is an Express Contract.

IMPLIED CONTRACTS are those the existence and terms of which are manifested by conduct; as, where a person enters a grocery store, asks for $1.00 worth of coffee, receives it, and walks away without saying anything about payment. It is implied that he will pay for the coffee, and he is as liable for the price of it as though he had expressly said that he would pay. Even where there is an Express Contract made, there are usually one or more Implied Contracts accompanying and connected with the transaction; as where a person makes an Express Contract for the purchase of groceries, it is in cities usually implied that the grocer will deliver the groceries, and also implied that the customer's house will be open to receive them during reasonable hours.

And, generally, there is the implied agreement in every transaction that the parties thereto will do whatever is necessary to make possible the carrying out of the conditions of the Contract.

WRITTEN CONTRACTS are those in which the terms of the Contract are set forth by means of handwriting, printing, or by any characters, on any material, with any instrument, and signed by the parties.

The particular advantage of Written Contracts is that the exact language assented to by the parties may be preserved for future reference; so it is important in writing a Contract to use such materials as will make the writing indelible and permanent. A Contract written in lead pencil is legal, but is easily altered.

ORAL CONTRACTS are those in which the Contract is entered into by means of spoken words. In general, Oral Contracts are equally as binding upon the parties as Written Contracts. (Exceptions will be noted in a subsequent chapter.)

The great advantage of Oral Contracts is in the ease with which they can be entered into. In matters of small consequence Oral Contracts are preferred to the formal written ones.

CONFLICTING CONTRACTS.—If a Contract in writing is made, and also an Oral Contract concerning the same object and between the same parties, which is materially different from the written agreement, the written agreement will control the Oral Contract. In so far as the Oral Contract is in conflict with the written one it is of no effect. The reason for this is that the Written Contract is presumed to be more carefully and formally made, and to be the result of deliberation, and therefore more nearly to express the real intentions of the parties than an oral one. For a like reason parts in handwriting control printed parts in a Contract.

ENTIRE CONTRACT.—An Entire Contract is one in which an entire performance on the part of one party must precede performance by the other; as where a carriage maker agrees to manufacture a certain carriage at a price of $100. The carriage must be fully completed before the maker can demand any part of the pay. A half-finished carriage would be of no use to the customer.

SEVERABLE CONTRACTS are those in which complete performance by one party is not necessary before anything can be required of the other. When the price is expressly apportioned by the Contract or the apportionment may be implied to each item to be performed, the Contract will generally be held to be severable; as in case a Contract is made for the purchase of ten tons of pig iron at $80 per ton. If only five tons were delivered the contractor could claim payment for the five tons at $80 per ton.

TEST QUESTIONS.

1. Name the essentials of every Contract.
2. State fully the difference between "Express" Contract and "Implied" Contract, and the advantage of each.
3. A agrees to build a house for $2,000, the money to be paid when the house is completed. A never completes the house. Can he draw any of the contract price? Explain fully.
4. A agreed with B. that B should deliver 100 tons of hay at $5 a ton to A. B delivered twenty tons and no more. Discuss the transaction fully as a Contract, and the remedies of each party.

CHAPTER III.

PARTIES TO CONTRACTS.

ALL PARTIES except those forbidden by law may contract about any legal object in a lawful manner, but there are exceptions expressly made by the Statute Law, as follows: "All persons are capable of contracting except—
(1) Minors;
(2) Persons of unsound mind; and
(3) Persons deprived of civil rights."
MINORS are:
(1) Males under 21 years of age;
(2) Females under 18 years of age;
and in computing the periods specified the time must be calculated from the first minute of the day on which persons are born to the same minute of the corresponding day completing the period of minority; that is, if a male child is born on the 10th day of March, at 6 o'clock A. M., he becomes of age on the 10th day of March, twenty-one years after, at one minute past 12 o'clock A. M.

In general, a minor's Contracts are considered valid until he wishes to avoid them, which he may do either before his majority or within a reasonable time afterwards. Some Contracts, however, especially declare a minor may not make, hence these are absolutely void from the beginning; as,

A Contract appointing an agent.

All other Contracts (not valid), however, are merely voidable. The marriage of a minor does not remove the disability of minority; that is, a minor who marries does not acquire any more rights and is not deprived of any rights whatever in regard to Contracts by reason of such marriage.

(16)

By a special Act of Legislature a marriage settlement given by a minor who is capable of contracting marriage is valid, and can not be afterwards avoided. A minor who falsely represents himself as being of full age can not afterwards avoid the Contract on the ground of his minority. This rule is in harmony with the legal maxim, "No one is allowed to take advantage of his own wrongful act."

PERSONS OF UNSOUND MIND.—This is quite a comprehensive term and includes idiots, lunatics, drunken persons, or persons who from great age, sickness, or other causes are not of sound mind. A person who claims that his contract is not valid because of his unsoundness of mind must show that his mind was unsound at the time of entering into the contract. The fact that he was of unsound mind before or after the date of entering into the contract would not be sufficient to relieve him in any degree from responsibility for his contract.

A person who enters into a contract while he is of unsound mind, may, when he is restored to sound mind, refuse to carry out his part of the contract, on the ground it was entered into while he was not capable of contracting. This sort of a contract, therefore, is said to be a Voidable Contract.

A person who has a monomania, that is, who is of unsound mind on one subject only, can not avoid any contract which he may make concerning other subjects.

If a person is an absolute idiot, his contract is absolutely void, and of no effect whatever. And where a person has been judicially declared insane, and a guardian appointed, his contracts are void even though made during a lucid interval.

DRUNKARDS.—Drunkenness is in itself no excuse for non-performance of a contract, and contracts entered into while under the influence of, or suffering from the effect of, intoxicating liquor, are only voidable when a person is so drunk as to seriously impair the reasoning faculties, or in other words, to make him of unsound mind.

It has been decided that where a person voluntarily becomes

2

intoxicated that he may enter into a contract and afterwards avoid it, such intoxication is no defense whatever against a person who wishes to compel him to perform his contract.

PERSONS DEPRIVED OF CIVIL RIGHTS are not absolutely debarred from making contracts, but may make them, and after they are released from prison or restored to their rights, they may avoid the contracts. In case of a person who is imprisoned for life, however, an exception is made. His contracts are considered valid.

DISAFFIRMANCE OF CONTRACTS.—A person is said to disaffirm a voidable contract when he refuses to be bound by its terms. The right of disaffirmance may be exerted by one who has entered into a contract while under disability. He is allowed a reasonable time after the disability is removed. As in the case of a minor, a man must disaffirm his contract within a reasonable time after becoming twenty-one years of age. Should the minor die before reaching his majority, the contract may be disaffirmed in the same manner in his behalf, by the administrator of his estate. What would be a reasonable time depends on the circumstances of each case.

In one case a minor sold a promissory note, received the purchase money, and endorsed the note to the purchaser, and for eleven months after she arrived at her majority, made no offer to return the purchase money or disaffirm the sale. It was held that eleven months was an unreasonable time, and she therefore could not recover the note.

Disaffirmance must be manifested by some positive act. The party disaffirming must do or say something to show that he avoids the contract. Thus it is held that where a minor grantor of land on attaining his majority executes another deed, this second deed will avoid the first.

AFFIRMANCE.—A voidable contract may be affirmed within a reasonable time after (not before) the disability is removed, either,

(1) By express ratification in words; or

(2) By acts which imply affirmance; or

(3) By omission to disaffirm.

We observe that disaffirmance must be more formal and explicit than affirmance. By merely saying or doing nothing a person will affirm a contract, while if he wishes to disaffirm, he must make it known in some positive manner.

The right of affirmance or disaffirmance is confined exclusively to the person who is under disability; so that while a minor has a right to disaffirm certain contracts, an adult who enters into the contract with the minor has no right to disaffirm.

CONTRACTS FOR NECESSARIES.—A minor or a person of unsound mind can not disaffirm a contract, otherwise valid, to pay the reasonable value of things necessary for his support or that of his family. This is an exception to the general rule of contracts stated above, and it is just in its operation, both to the person under disability and those dealing with him.

It is necessary, however, that the credit be given to the minor or incompetent person himself, otherwise he is not chargeable, though he has received the articles. Reasonable value is a question of fact and would ordinarily be the market value of the goods at the time they were furnished.

NECESSARIES OF LIFE are:

(1) Proper food;

(2) Clothing;

(3) Lodging;

(4) Medical attendance;

(5) Education.

What is necessary depends on a person's station in life, and is not restricted to what is absolutely necessary merely to support life. A person with a large estate can bind himself to pay for more expensive clothes, better food and lodging, and a higher education, than a poor person. Each case must be determined according to its own circumstances. In one case kid gloves, silk cravats, walking canes, and cologne, were held not to be necessaries. Generally, luxurious articles of utility may be included under the term "necessaries," *e. g.*, a watch; while luxurious articles which are purely ornamental are not included as necessaries, *e. g.*, ear-rings; and even an article which is considered necessary for persons in any station in life, such as flour, would not be a necessary if a person were already well supplied with flour; and a dealer furnishing such person with unusual quantities of flour could not recover pay for more than was required for ordinary use.

ALIEN ENEMIES.—In the event of war breaking out between the United States and a foreign country all business is suspended between the countries, and every subject of the foreign country is considered an enemy; hence, by furnishing goods to a merchant in the foreign country, a merchant of the United States would be aiding the enemy; therefore all such contracts are absolutely void.

* * *

TEST QUESTIONS.

1. Who are competent parties to a contract?
2. Distinguish between "void" and "voidable" contracts.
3. A minor orphan contracts a bill for butter and flour, and is sued for the price. He pleads infancy as a defense. In whose favor should the Court decide?
4. A farm hand wrote and signed a promissory note. Upon being sued for the amount, he alleges intoxication as a defense. Can he defeat the suit upon such plea?
5. A person enters into a contract and afterwards becomes insane. The contract being otherwise valid, how may it be enforced against his estate?
6. Illustrate fully the manner in which a contract may be "affirmed" or "disaffirmed."
7. Name the "necessaries of life" and illustrate what articles would or would not be "necessaries" under certain circumstances.

CHAPTER IV.

CONSENT OF PARTIES.

CONSENT is the agreement by the parties to a contract concerning the object of the contract, and must be *free, mutual,* and *communicated by each to the other.* Until there is an agreement containing these three elements, there is no consent to the contract.

A PROPOSAL or offer must, of course, be made by one party wishing to enter into a contract. This does not bind the person who makes the offer until his offer is accepted, and he may withdraw it at any time before acceptance. The rule is that an oral proposition must be accepted at the time it is made, or at furthest, before the parties separate. If they separate without having entered into the contract, the offer can not be accepted later unless time was expressly given.

In case of a written proposal being made a reasonable time is allowed for acceptance or refusal, and what a reasonable time is must be determined by the circumstances of each case.

ACCEPTANCE.—The parties must. agree upon the same thing in the same sense, in order to make a valid contract; hence the acceptance must be absolute and unqualified. If it contains any conditions it is not a valid acceptance, but amounts in effect to a new proposal; as if A offers to sell a typewriter to B for $100 cash, and B replies, saying, "I will accept your offer if you will take my note instead of the cash." B thus makes a new offer, which may be accepted by A or not, as he pleases.

WRITTEN PROPOSALS.—In case a proposal is sent by letter, the offer remains open until the letter in the usual course of mail would reach its destination, and for a reasonable time thereafter.

(21)

The acceptance of a written offer takes effect as soon as the party accepting it has put his acceptance in the course of transmission to the proposer, even though the proposer may not receive the acceptance for a long time, or may not receive it at all.

This may seem to work a hardship on the proposer, but he may limit the time for holding his offer open for acceptance in this manner: "If I do not hear from you within ten days I shall conclude you do not accept." This would relieve him from holding open the offer more than ten days even though an acceptance had been mailed within the ten days and not received until after the ten days had elapsed.

In case an offer is sent by mail, and within proper time is accepted by mail, we have seen that from the moment the letter of acceptance is started, the acceptance is complete, therefore, if the proposer changes his mind and mails a letter withdrawing the offer before the acceptance reaches him, the acceptance is nevertheless effective and the contract is complete.

IMPLIED GENERAL PROPOSALS.—Every storekeeper by placing goods on his shelves and opening his doors to the public, thereby invites every one to come in and make purchases, and any person may enter such store and demand any article therein displayed on tender of the proper price. This is the acceptance of the general proposal, and when thus accepted the contract is complete.

CONSENT, VOIDABLE.—A consent which is obtained by

(1) Duress;

(2) Menace;

(3) Fraud;

(4) Undue influence; or

(5) Mistake;

is not free, and the contract is therefore voidable on the ground of lack of consent.

DURESS consists in

(1) Unlawful confinement of a person or his relatives;

(2) The unlawful detention of his property; as where a person holds a sum of money and refuses to deliver it until a contract is entered into. And under the first subdivision above, one who pays money for his release from prison under unlawful confinement, may recover the money so paid.

MENACE consists of a threat of unlawful injury to the person or character or property of a person, made with the intent of compelling consent to a contract. A person who enters into a contract under such menace, may avoid the contract on that ground, and if he has paid anything, may recover everything he has paid by reason of the threat made. It must be remembered that the threat must be of unlawful prosecution. A threat of lawful prosecution against a person will not constitute duress; and a person claiming duress must show not only that he was in fear, but that he had reasonable grounds for believing that he or his property was in actual danger.

FRAUD, generally, is said to be some deception practised with the intent of inducing a person to enter into a contract. This, however, is not strictly correct. In order to constitute fraud in a legal sense it is necessary that material damage should be done by reason of the deception.

No matter what false statements or representations are made to a person, if he does not believe them, and is not deceived thereby to his injury, he can not claim to have been defrauded; and he is bound to use such diligence as an ordinarily prudent business man would use in entering into contracts, otherwise he can not avoid the contract on the ground of fraud, as the law will not assist any one who is defrauded by reason of his own negligence or foolishness.

Nevertheless, if, as in the case of a man buying a horse, the person relies entirely on the dealer's judgment, stating that he knows nothing about a horse and wishes a gentle, well-broken animal, and the dealer by wilful falsehood assures him that the horse is all that is desired, when in fact he is not, the purchaser is entitled to avoid the contract, return the horse, and receive back his money on the ground of fraud.

CRIMINAL LIABILITY.—A person who defrauds another, or who makes any contract or conveyance with the attempt to defraud or deceive, or to hinder or delay creditors in the collection of their just debts, is, under the provisions of the Penal Code, guilty of a misdemeanor, and may be punished by fine and imprisonment, in addition to any civil liability in damages to the injured party.

UNDUE INFLUENCE consists in taking an unfair advantage of another's weakness of mind, or necessities, or distress, or by using a person's confidence unduly to induce him to enter into contracts; as where a child would take advantage of an aged father's weakness of mind to induce him to disinherit other children. Undue influence, however, must be carefully distinguished from the ordinary influence which is brought to bear by one person upon another in every-day life for the purpose of inducing the making of contracts. Just what amount of weakness of mind or distress on the part of one party, and what amount of influence exerted on the part of the other party, will constitute undue influence, so as to make the contract voidable, is a question of fact to be determined by the circumstances of each case. In any event, the influence so exerted must have resulted in damage to the person influenced, otherwise the contract can not be avoided.

MISTAKE is,

(1) An unconscious ignorance of a fact material to the contract; or

(2) A belief in the existence of a thing material to a contract, which does not exist.

It is absolutely necessary that the mistake be mutual; therefore mistake, under the law of contracts, means something entirely different from what is ordinarily meant by the term.

If the misapprehension is only on the part of one party, the other party knowing full well concerning the matter, it amounts to a deception on the part of the party having such knowledge; as if A thinks he is selling a tract of land, other than that actually conveyed, and B thinks that he is receiving that which is conveyed, it is a mutual mistake; but if A knows he is selling a tract of land other than that B thinks is conveyed, it is a fraud on A's part, and not a mistake. To take advantage of mistake, reasonable diligence must be used in avoiding the contract by the party who is injured, and he must return anything which he has received under the contract before he can avoid it.

TEST QUESTIONS.

1. Name three elements constituting consent.
2. A physician buys a horse from a dealer for use in his profession; the horse proves to be vicious and refuses to stand. Under what circumstances would the contract be voidable, and under what valid?
3. A man purchases an article for a certain but unexpressed purpose; it proves to be unfit for such purpose. May he return the article and rescind the contract?
4. Distinguish critically between "mistake" and "fraud" in law of contracts.

CHAPTER V.

CONSIDERATION.

CONSIDERATION.—In all contracts there is in reality a consideration offered by each party to the other to induce him to enter into the contract. For convenience, however, money, or its equivalent, is usually spoken of as the consideration in ordinary contracts, and the thing, other than money, is called the object of the contract.

As a general rule all contracts require a consideration, but there are two exceptions.

(1) Negotiable paper in the hands of an innocent purchaser for value before maturity.

(2) Certain mutual promises, as mutual promises to marry.

VALUABLE CONSIDERATION consists of—

(1) Any benefit to the promisor.

(2) Loss or inconvenience to the promisee.

It is not therefore necessarily money which is the consideration, but any benefit, and the word "any" includes the smallest benefit which is of value. The law does not presume to say what is the reasonable value of an article.

Examples.—In the absence of fraud, or other legal reason for avoiding the contract, a person who sells a fine horse for $5.00 must abide by his contract. He can not avoid it on the ground of the inadequacy of the consideration.

An agreement to pay in future greater interest on a note, is sufficient consideration for the agreement of the creditor not to sue.

The part payment of a note when all is due is not sufficient consideration for a promise to extend the time of payment.

(26)

GOOD CONSIDERATION consists of the love and affection which near relatives have toward each other. A man deeds his son a house and lot without any valuable consideration—merely as a gift. The love inducing the gift would be a good consideration. Such consideration will only be sufficient after the gift has been made. A mere promise to give something in the future, even to a child, can not be enforced.

It is the duty of a father, mother or child of any poor person, who is unable to maintain himself, by working, to maintain such person to the extent of their ability, and the promise of an adult child to pay for necessaries previously furnished to a parent is binding. The law in such cases presumes the love and affection which makes the good consideration.

CREDITOR'S RIGHTS.—While it is true that as between the parties to a contract, a small consideration, or the consideration of love and affection, may be sufficient to support a contract, nevertheless, if a person deeds valuable property for an extremely small sum to a friend, with the understanding that it is to be reconveyed to him, and this contract is made for the purpose of defrauding his creditors, the conveyance may be set aside, and the contract declared void in a suit brought by the creditors. The same is true in case a man gives his property to his relatives in order to prevent his creditors from enforcing their just claims; and in general, when there are creditors, the conveyance of property for a small or no consideration, is considered good evidence of fraud.

ANY CONSIDERATION which is perversive of the letter or intent of the law, is an unlawful consideration, and will not support a contract; as A gives B his note on the consideration that B will procure A's escape from jail, B can not collect anything on the note because the releasing of prisoners in such manner is unlawful.

IMPOSSIBLE.—Everything is deemed possible which is possible in the nature of things. A man who has agreed to pay

$100 as consideration for services performed can not avoid payment on the ground of impossibility by saying that it is impossible for him to pay the hundred dollars. It is not impossible in the nature of things. A mere pecuniary impossibility is not a legal impossibility.

When the consideration is on its face impossible of execution, the entire contract is void; as where the consideration is that A shall travel from San Francisco to New York in a day.

FAILING.—If the consideration is apparently sufficient, but in fact worthless, or if sufficient when the contract is made, and subsequently becomes of no value, this failure of consideration will make void the entire contract; as where a person receives shares of stock in a mining company, and afterwards discovers that the certificate of stock has been forged.

TEST QUESTIONS.

1. A man in contemplation of insolvency conveys his property to his son. May his creditors enforce payment from that property?

2. A agrees to give B $100 to leave the state until a certain case is tried so as not to be a witness. B does so and returns. A refuses to pay the $100. Discuss the remedies of B.

CHAPTER VI.

THE OBJECT.

THE OBJECT of a contract is the thing which it is agreed on the part of the party receiving the consideration to do, or not to do; or in other words, it is the thing about which the agreement is made; as in the case of the purchase of a horse, the horse is the object of the contract.

LAWFUL.—The object of the contract must be lawful when the contract is made, and possible and ascertainable by the time the contract is to be performed.

Where a contract has but a single object, and such object is unlawful, the entire contract is void; but where a contract has several distinct objects, if one is lawful and the others unlawful, the contract is valid in regard to the lawful object, and void as to the rest; as where a person gives a mortgage securing an individual note, and a company note, if the company note is void, the mortgage security will nevertheless be good as securing the individual note.

UNLAWFUL.—That is not lawful which is

(1) Contrary to an express provision of law;

(2) Contrary to public policy;

(3) Otherwise contrary to good morals.

Under the definition in subdivision one, it makes no difference in the validity of the contract that the contract is not criminal in its nature. It is enough if it is contrary to the provisions of law; as if a man agrees for a consideration to drive a horse through the streets of a city at the rate of fifteen miles per hour; fast driving being prohibited, the contract would be invalid, even though in itself there is no wrong in driving a horse at a rapid rate.

(29)

If payment is refused under such a contract, the driver can not recover the consideration in a suit at law, because the contract is unlawful, and in accordance with the legal maxim, "The law will not aid wrongdoers."

Under subdivision two, it has been decided that agreements in consideration of aiding a candidate to procure an office, to share the salary of the office, are contrary to public policy and therefore void; as is a contract to keep a witness for the government out of the way until after a trial is over. In either of these cases no part of the contract can be enforced.

CONTRACTS IN RESTRAINT OF TRADE also come within the purview of subdivision two above, as being against public policy. It often happens that a person builds up a profitable business, and people are attracted to his place of business by reason of his personal qualities. If he sells out his business to a stranger, it is customary for the stranger to require a contract from him to the effect that he will not open another store for the transaction of the same kind of business, as he would probably by so doing take many of his regular customers away from the stranger. Such contracts, however, are not void, provided the seller agrees to refrain from carrying on a similar business within the limits of a specified county, city, or part thereof; and even such a contract is only valid so long as the buyer, or any person deriving title to the good-will from him, carries on a like business therein.

It is held that where A agreed not to carry on the business of street paving in the city of San Francisco, or the state of California, that the entire contract was void as including more territory than allowed by law.

A contract which does not specify any territorial limit at all, is, of course, void; as, where a contract was entered into not to engage in "any branch of the yeast powder business," the contract was held to be absolutely void.

In regard to partners, however, the limit within which any

outgoing partner may carry on a similar business on dissolution is the boundary of the city or town where the partnership business has been transacted, or a specified part therein. The theory upon which contracts of restraint of trade are allowed at all, is that the buyer is entitled to the good-will of the business. Good-will is the expectation of continued public patronage. Our law-makers have concluded that in the ordinary lines of business a man can not expect patronage from a larger extent of territory than one county, hence that limit has been fixed.

CONTRACTS RESTRAINING MARRIAGE.—Every contract in restraint of the marriage of any person other than a minor is void; but this does not affect limitations where the intent was not to forbid marriage, but only to give the use until marriage; thus a contract by which a father agrees to give his son one thousand dollars if he does not marry until he is twenty-one years of age, is in all respects valid; but if the contract is that the son shall forfeit all claim to his inheritance if he marries at any time, it is invalid; but where a widow is given the use of certain property until she remarries, the condition is valid, as merely giving the use until marriage and not forbidding marriage.

BROKERAGE CONTRACTS are in all cases void. The proprietor of a so-called marriage bureau can not enforce the collection of any fee agreed to be paid him for negotiating a marriage, as the contract in itself is against public policy, in that it encourages marriage of persons hastily, and as a mere matter of business speculation.

FRAUDULENT CONTRACTS.—All contracts which have for their object an exemption of any one from responsibility for his own fraud, or for fraudulent injury to the person or property of another, are against the policy of the law, and therefore void; as for example, where a debtor in failing circumstances makes a transfer of his property to a friend for the purpose of defrauding his creditors, such contract is absolutely void in all respects, and creditors may recover the property and have it applied to the satisfaction of their debts, upon proving that fraud has been committed.

The debtor himself, however, is bound by the act of transferring the property to his friend, and can not compel the friend to give back the property, as he himself committed fraud, and the law will not aid wrongdoers. The law provides, however, that a debtor may make assignments of his property to any person in trust for the benefit of his creditors. This act when done without fraud is valid, and any surplus that may remain after his creditors are paid, the assignee must return to the debtor. Under what is termed the National Bankruptcy Law, which is in force in all the states and territories, creditors, upon proper application to the Court, may compel the placing of his property in the hands of an assignee for the purpose of being sold to satisfy their claims. Any assignments, if voluntary, must place all creditors on an equal footing. So far as the assignment gives one creditor a larger share than another it is void, as being a fraud upon other creditors.

CONTRARY TO GOOD MORALS.—A note given by a wife for land conveyed to her by her husband in consideration of her allowing him to get a divorce, has been held void, as being contrary to good morals. Obscene publications come under the head of immoral contracts, and consequently any such contracts are void, and the price agreed to be paid can not be recovered in a suit at law; and under the Penal Code any person who writes, composes, distributes, sells, or publishes any lewd paper, picture, or figure, or sings any lewd or obscene song in public, is guilty of a misdemeanor, and his contract for performance of any such acts is absolutely void.

Wagers are against good morals, and will not be enforced by the Courts; however, it has been held that before the wager has been decided by the stake-holder either party may recover his money from the stake-holder, but that after the money has been paid by him to one of the parties, the transaction is complete, and the money so paid can not be recovered.

It has been held that where a purse is offered by way of premium or reward, for the winner of a horse-race, it does not come within the law against bets or wagers, and the contract may be enforced.

SUNDAY CONTRACTS.—In many of the states there are laws against making contracts on Sunday, and the impression is so general that it is necessary to state that in California there is no Sunday law, and, consequently, any contracts which would be valid on any other day of the week would be valid on Sunday. Even contracts which would appear to be in desecration of the Sabbath, such as a contract to play ball on Sunday, are valid, and the ball player may collect his wages for his services performed on Sunday, if his claim is otherwise valid. Sunday is, however, a legal holiday, and certain acts relating to business of the state and the Courts are not valid if performed on that day; not because it is Sunday, but because it is a legal holiday.

ELEMENTS OF FRAUD.—As has been stated in a previous chapter, a mere falsehood is not necessarily a fraud, and the following elements must all be represented in a contract before the contract can be declared void on the ground of fraud.

(1) The means resorted to must be for the purpose of inducing the one deceived to enter the contract.

(2) They must be false in fact.

(3) The party resorting to them must have had no belief in them, or no reasonable ground for believing them.

(4) The party deceived must have relied upon them, and been justified in relying upon them.

(5) There must have been material damage to the party deceived.

From the fourth element it will be seen that a person must exert at least ordinary care in accepting any statements as true, otherwise he can not claim to have been defrauded.

In the case of a sale of wool which had been exposed to a rainstorm in order to make it weigh heavier, the seller explained the

3

stains on the sacks caused by the water by saying that they were old sacks. It was held that the purchaser exerted due diligence; that all the elements of fraud were present, and that he was entitled to rescind the contract and receive back what he paid for the wool.

TEST QUESTIONS.

1. A baseball player contracts to play a certain game on Sunday, for a consideration. May he collect the sum agreed upon?
2. A marriage broker procures a wife for A and sues him for a fee of $50. Can he recover judgment? Give reasons.
3. A sells his store to B and agrees not to open another store in the same line of business. Discuss the validity of the agreement.
4. A agrees to give his daughter $5.000 on her eighteenth birthday if she remains unmarried until that time. Can she recover the $5,000 before that time? Give reasons.

CHAPTER VII.

INTERPRETATION, NOVATION, AND CANCELLATION.

Even though a contract may have been entered into by formal and carefully-drawn writing, or by the most explicit oral understanding, yet it often happens that the meaning is not plain, and has been understood differently by the respective parties; hence certain rules have been laid down for the interpretation of contracts; and, in general, all contracts are to be interpreted by the same rules.

MUTUAL INTENTIONS.—A contract must be interpreted so as to give effect to the mutual intention of the parties as it existed at the time of contracting, so far as the same is ascertainable and lawful. Of course, so far as any part of the contract is unlawful, it is void and of no effect. The language of a contract is to govern its interpretation, if the language is clear and explicit, and does not involve an absurdity. In a case where a bond was given the intention was to have it read "two thousand two hundred dollars." The word "thousand" was omitted, and it read "two two hundred dollars." The Court decided that the language did involve an absurdity, there being no such thing as "two two hundred dollars," and that therefore oral evidence would be admitted to show what was intended.

WRITTEN CONTRACTS.—When a contract is reduced to writing, the intention of the parties is to be ascertained from the writing alone, unless, through fraud, mistake, or accident it fails to express the real intention of the parties; as in a case where a man who could not read was asked to sign a promissory note with the understanding that it provided for the payment by him of $100. In fact the note provided for the payment of $500. The Court held that oral evidence of the intention might be given, and the contract was declared void on the ground of fraud. The execution of a contract in writing, whether the law requires it to be written or not, supersedes all oral agreements concerning the same matter, which preceded or accompanied it. Effect is to be given to every part of a contract if reasonably practicable, and the whole contract is to be taken together in construing the meaning, and not by parts; and where there are several contracts relating to the same matters between the same parties, they are to be taken together as parts of the one transaction; as in cases where a number of letters have been written containing proposals and acceptances, all of the letters will be read together as forming one contract, the parts of the letters containing rejected proposals being rejected from the contract.

TECHNICAL WORDS.—The words of a contract are to be understood in their ordinary and popular sense, rather than according to their strict legal meaning, unless they are used by the parties in a technical sense; and such technical words are to be interpreted as usually understood by persons in the business or profession to which they relate. A word which is used with a particular meaning in one portion of a contract is presumed to have been used in like sense in other places.

The word "stubble," as used in a lease, was held to be a technical word, including grain remaining uncut after the period of harvest, as well as the straw from which the grain had been cut, it being shown that that was the meaning as usually understood by farmers in that section of the country.

LAW OF PLACE.—A contract is to be interpreted according to the law and usage of the place where it is to be performed, or if no place of performance is specified, then according to the law and usage of the place where it is made. Mere usage, however, can not be admitted in evidence to destroy the plain meaning of a contract. A contract may be perfectly valid, even though in its terms it declares things which are contrary to the ordinary usage;

but evidence of usage is used as an instrument of interpretation only; as in the case of the word "stubble" in the case cited above, the decision was based partly on the usage of the place as to the meaning of the word "stubble."

REPUGNANCIES.—Where different clauses of the same contract are in conflict with each other, they must be reconciled, if possible, by such interpretation as will give some effect to the repugnant clauses. Where, however, there is a flat contradiction between different parts, that in handwriting controls printed parts, and special statements control general statements. Written statements control oral declarations. Parts purely original control those copied from a printed form. In cases of uncertainty which still exist after the foregoing rules are applied, the language of the contract must be interpreted most strongly against the party who caused the uncertainty to exist. If A agreed to work for a day, he writing the agreement himself, in case it was uncertain as to what the word "day" meant, it would be construed to mean the longest working day rather than the shortest.

TIME.—If no time is specified for the performance of an act required to be performed, a reasonable time is allowed. If the act is in its nature capable of being done immediately, as, for example, if it consists in the payment of money only, it must be performed immediately upon the thing to be done being exactly ascertained. The word "immediately" does not mean within any particular minute or hour, but as soon as, with ordinary diligence, the act can be accomplished. What a reasonable time is depends upon the circumstances of each case.

In one case where A agreed to convey certain lands, his failure to do so within eight years was held to be an unreasonable length of time, and the contract was broken by reason of such failure.

NOVATION is the substitution of a new obligation for an existing one, and is made,

(1) By substituting a new obligation;

(2) By substituting a new debtor; or

(3) By substituting a new creditor.

Novation is made by contract, and is subject to all the rules concerning contracts in general.

CANCELLATION.—A contract not in writing may be altered in any respect by consent of the parties in writing without a new consideration, and the original contract is cancelled thereby to the extent of the new alteration. ＾

A contract in writing may be altered by a contract in writing or by an executed oral agreement, and not otherwise; as for example, if by a written contract A agrees to sell B a horse for fifty dollars, the parties may alter the written contract by writing "one hundred dollars," or they may orally agree that the price shall be one hundred dollars, and as soon as the hundred dollars is paid and the horse delivered, the original contract is canceled.

Destruction intentionally caused by a party entitled to benefit under the contract, or with his consent, extinguishes all the obligations of the contract in his favor, and in any case the destruction of a written contract with the intent to extinguish the obligations thereof, extinguishes the contract as to all parties consenting to the act.

TEST QUESTIONS.

1. A railroad company took a cable rope from the manufacturers with the understanding that it was to be kept and paid for if satisfactory. The company returned the rope to the manufacturers. The manufacturers sued for the price. Were they entitled to recover?

2. A entered into a written contract with B by which he was to pay $100 for goods. A admitted that he had signed the writing and knew what it contained at the time, but stated that there was an oral agreement at the time that

he was only to pay $75 for the goods. In case of suit will he be compelled to pay $75 or $100? Give reasons.

3. In the above case suppose that A could not read and was informed that the consideration was $75. Would he be compelled to pay the $100?

4. A agreed to rent to B a "spike" team. On a trial for damage for refusal to furnish the team, A claimed that a "spike" team meant two horses for hauling spikes; B contended that it meant three horses for any purpose. State different circumstances which would decide the case for one party or the other.

CHAPTER VIII.

REMEDIES.

DEFINITION.—In every contract, as we have seen, there are mutual promises by the parties thereto. If all of these promises were at all times faithfully kept and performed there would be no damage done and consequently no redress required, but it is the common experience of mankind that contracts are often broken. We have from the old common law the maxim, "There is no wrong without a remedy." Remedies are obtained by application to the Courts by means of what is called a suit or action at law.

SUIT is commenced by filing a written statement called a complaint in Court, setting forth the contract, and that it has been broken, and the damage claimed by reason of the breach of contract.

A summons, or notice, is then issued commanding the one who has broken the contract to appear within a certain time named, and make answer to the complaint against him. After he does this, the trial is had and the Court or jury determines whether the contract has been broken, and if so what relief is proper.

The Order made by the Court stating the relief that is granted is called the judgment, and this judgment of the Court is enforced by a Sheriff or Constable, and is called the execution of the judgment. Judgment may be for specific performance, injunction, or for damages.

EXECUTION.—Where the judgment is for damages, the Sheriff or Constable may seize the real and personal property of the debtor and sell it. If there is any surplus, he must return it to the debtor, but he must be careful to sell personal property

(40)

first, then real property, and only so much as is necessary to satisfy the judgment. Execution may issue any time within five years from entry of judgment.

EXEMPTIONS.—As a matter of public policy, it would not be good policy to allow a creditor to take every article which the debtor owns away from him in satisfaction of his debts, as it might effectually prevent him from earning his livelihood, and thereby create a class of paupers who would be a burden on the general public; hence, the general rule is, that whatever is necessary for the actual earning of a person's livelihood, or for his ordinary use, is exempt from execution. The following are illustrations of what is exempt:—

(1) Necessary household and office furniture.

(2) Necessary farming utensils; not exceeding in value $1,000; also two work animals, harness and wagon.

(3) All public property, such as jails, court-houses and town halls.

(4) The library of an attorney, the piano of a music teacher, the typewriter of a stenographer, the horses and dray of a drayman, and other like things by which a debtor earns his living.

DAMAGES.—In case a party to a contract fails to fulfil his agreements, and a suit is brought and judgment entered, this judgment usually provides that he must pay a certain sum of money as damages to the injured party.

In general the damages allowed is the amount which will compensate for all the injury suffered.

DIRECT AND CONSEQUENTIAL DAMAGES.—Damage must be the natural and proximate result of an act in order that compensation in money may be obtained. There are only two classes of cases where injuries have been sustained for which damages may be allowed. The injury must be:—

(1) Direct; that is, such as proceeds immediately from the act, or,

(2) Consequential; such as flows necessarily from the act; for example:

A killed a mare. The damage sustained was direct damage in the loss of the animal. She had an unweaned colt. The cost of employing other means to raise the colt was consequential damage, and the owner of the mare recovered as damages the value of the mare, and the additional expense of raising the colt. The additional injury caused by the colt kicking its keeper was too remote to charge A. The kicking was neither the direct result of the killing of the mare, nor did it necessarily result therefrom. The colt might have kicked the man had the mother lived.

SPECULATIVE DAMAGES.—Damages must always be either direct or consequential; and they must also be certain. If a man makes a mere supposition or speculation that he has been damaged, he can not recover damages. In the above example, the extra price which the colt might have brought, had it been reared by the mother, is mere speculation, and not recoverable. No one can tell whether the colt would have been of more value had the mother lived, or not.

LIQUIDATED, OR FIXED DAMAGES.—In some contracts it is found that, owing to the nature of the contract, it is very difficult to say what amount of damages will compensate for a breach thereof. When from the nature of the case it would be impracticable or extremely difficult to fix the actual damage after it occurs, the parties may agree beforehand upon an amount which shall be allowed as damages to the injured party in case the contract is broken. This agreement is usually made a part of the contract itself. but it may be specified in a separate instrument.

A purchased a sailing vessel from F. F agreed to deliver the vessel within twenty days, and it was agreed that if he did not he should pay $2,000 as damages to A. He failed to deliver, and on suit being brought, the Court held that it was one of the cases in which it was extremely difficult or impracticable to fix the actual damages, and therefore allowed the $2,000 agreed upon as damages. In the ordinary cases, however, where the damage can be ascertained, fixed damages are not allowed.

EXEMPLARY DAMAGES are damages which are allowed in addition to any actual damage suffered in cases where there has been wilful injury inflicted. Such damages, however, are never allowed for mere breach of contract, but only in cases of wilful or malicious injury. Such wilful wrongs are called torts, and additional damages by way of example, or exemplary damages, are allowed in such cases, except in cases where a person by reason of being of unsound mind or a minor is not capable of knowing that the act is wrongful. If a person commits wrongful injury to animals, such as maliciously leaving horses to starve, or die from want of water, exemplary damages may be given in addition to damages for the actual value of the horses.

In contracts for the payment of money only, the damage caused by the breach thereof is deemed to be the amount due with interest thereon. The actual loss occasioned by the breach of such a contract may be much greater than the amount due with interest, but the law does not inquire into consequences which may arise beyond the amount due with interest.

BREACH OF CONTRACT TO DELIVER PERSONAL PROPERTY.—If the property has not been paid for, the damage caused by the breach of contract on the part of the seller is the difference between the value of the property to the buyer, and the price he has agreed to pay; as, if a fruit dealer bought at wholesale certain apples for $50 and they were not delivered, and he had a contract for their sale for $75, his damage caused by the non-delivery of the apples would be the difference between $50 and $75, or $25.

If the personal property has been paid for and not delivered the amount of the damages is either,

(1) The value of the property at the time it should have been delivered, with legal interest; or

(2) The highest market value of the property at any time up to the time verdict is given in a suit for the recovery of damages.

BREACH OF CONTRACT TO PAY FOR PERSONAL PROPERTY SOLD.—Where a buyer breaks his contract and fails to accept and pay for personal property which he has bought, the damage to the seller is the amount of the contract price, and the seller may store the goods for him, and sue him for the contract price.

BREACH OF CONTRACT TO BUY PERSONAL PROPERTY.—In case the title has not passed, but there is a mere agreement to buy upon delivery, if the buyer refuses to accept and pay for personal property the seller may;

(1) Resell the property and recover as damages the amount of the difference between what he sold for and what the buyer has agreed to pay him; or,

(2) He may keep the goods and recover as damages whatever profit he would have made by the sale plus the expenses incurred in handling the goods.

EMPLOYEE WRONGFULLY DISCHARGED may recover damages which he may suffer by reason thereof. He may either

(1) Regard the contract as broken and sue at once for the breach, and may recover the profits that would have been made had the contract been fulfilled; or

(2) Treat the contract as rescinded and sue for the reasonable value of his services from the time he commenced work until the contract would have been completed.

In either case he must use ordinary diligence in looking for other employment, and in case he secures other employment at less wages, his damage will be the difference between what he does receive, and what he would have received under his contract.

It must be carefully remembered, however, that such damages are only obtainable in case an employee is wrongfully discharged. If he has been discharged by reason of failure to properly perform his duties he has no remedy, and if he has injured his employer by reason of his negligence or unskilful performance of his duties, the employer may recover damages from him.

SPECIFIC PERFORMANCE is the compelling of a person

to carry out the terms of his contract in case he refuses or neglects to do so. It is the general rule, as we have seen, that where contracts are broken the person who commits the breach of contract is made to pay damages in money to the other for the breach thereof, but there are some cases in which it is considered that mere money damages will not compensate a person for a breach of contract; and in such cases a judgment will be given compelling the full or specific performance of the contract.

As to the classes of contracts, the rule is that a breach of contract concerning personal property may be relieved by money damages; while if a person agrees to convey real property and fails to do so the Court will compel him to do so upon application by the injured party. In such a case, however, the party injured by the breach of contract must himself perform, or be compellable to perform, his part of the contract, in accordance with the maxim, "He who seeks equity must do equity."

A person who applies to the Court for a judgment for specific performance must do so within a reasonable time after the breach of contract. In one case where six years had elapsed the Court held that the injured party had waited an unreasonable length of time, and refused to compel a specific performance by the other. What a reasonable time is, however, depends upon the circumstances of each case.

AN INJUNCTION is a writ or order requiring a person to refrain from a particular act. It sometimes happens that a person inflicts injury upon the property of another, or threatens to do so; and to await the slow process of an ordinary suit at law might result in irreparable injury to the property; therefore when there is no plain, speedy and adequate remedy at law a person injured may apply to a Court for an injunction.

Injunction was held to be the proper remedy in the following cases:

A tenant was digging up fruit trees; an injunction was granted to compel him to stop.

An ex-sheriff was restrained from collecting taxes, by injunction. A person attempted to divert all the water from a miner's ditch. An injunction was issued to compel him to cease.

TEST QUESTIONS.

1. Name the various stages of an action for a debt.
2. A agrees to build a ship for B, and in case he fails to complete the work he is to forfeit $10,000 as damages. Is that part of the contract valid? Give reasons.
3. A enters into a contract with B for the purchase of B's land. At the time fixed for the performance B refuses to convey. What remedy or remedies has A?
4. A agreed to keep certain horses in pasture at a certain price. The horses died from lack of food and water in the pasture field. What damages may be recovered by the owner?

CHAPTER IX.

DEFENSES—STATUTE OF FRAUDS.

DEFINITION.—It sometimes happens that a person sues another for breach of contract through mistake, there having been in fact no breach of contract, or it may happen that the contract has been partly performed, or there may be some legal reason for not performing the contract. When a person has any such reasons he may offer them as defenses to the action against him. A defense, then, is a legal reason given by the defendant tending to show that there is no case against him.

The principal defenses are:—

(1) Statute of frauds;

(2) Statute of limitations;

(3) Performance;

(4) Counter claim.

THE STATUTE OF FRAUDS has for its object the prevention of fraud in contracts by requiring certain contracts to be in writing. The statute provides that the following contracts are invalid unless the same or some note or memorandum thereof be in writing, and subscribed by the party to be charged, or by its agent.

(1) An agreement that by its terms is not to be performed within a year;

(2) A promise to answer for the debt, default, or miscarriage of another.

(3) An agreement made upon consideration of marriage except mutual promises to marry.

(4) An agreement for the sale of personal property for a price of $200 or over, unless

(*a*) The buyer accepts or receives part of the thing; or,

(*b*) The buyer pays at the time part of the price; or

(*c*) The sale be by auction.

(5) An agreement for leasing real property for more than one year.

(6) An agreement for the sale of real property.

(7) An agreement employing an agent to purchase or sell real property.

EXPLANATION.—It has been found by experience that in matters of small consequence people are likely to fulfil their contracts, and less dispute consequently arises as to the meaning of such contracts. It would be very inconvenient, moreover, if a person were required to write out a contract every time he wished to make a trifling purchase, so the law has particularly specified, as above stated, what contracts are considered important enough to reduce to writing, and by thus reducing them to writing the interpretation is made reasonably certain.

Of course, the statute does not mean by the word "invalid" that a person who orally enters into such contracts as are required to be in writing, is guilty of any crime, or that he will be criminally liable for his act.

In so far as each party carries out the contract, and no one is injured, the statute does not apply and the contract is valid; in other words the statute does not actually make the contract void, but simply prevents any party who may be injured by breach of the contract from obtaining any remedy by suit at law if the other party sets up the statute as a defense for non-performance.

"Note or memorandum" must be full enough plainly to describe the contract and the parties thereto.

"Subscribed" means written at the end of the instrument. Mere signing of the name in or on some other part of the contract will not do.

"By the party to be charged." The other party need not subscribe his name. It is not necessary to state the consideration in the writing.

"BY ITS TERMS NOT TO BE PERFORMED WITHIN A YEAR."—The words "by its terms" are particularly important. If it does not appear by its terms that the agreement is not to be performed within a year from the making of it, the contract may be made orally and be valid in all respects. It is only when by its terms it expressly states that it is not to be performed within a year, or that fact otherwise appears by the terms of the contract, that the contract must be in writing; thus, a verbal contract was entered into to deliver saw logs sufficient to keep a sawmill running for two years. It was held that *by its terms* the contract was not to be performed within a year, and hence not being in writing the contract was invalid, and when the lumberman failed to furnish the logs, the owner of the sawmill could not recover damages, nor had he any remedy of any kind.

If the contract may be performed within a year it need not be in writing under any circumstances even though it actually takes longer than the year to perform it. As, if A agrees to build a carriage and to begin work immediately, the contract is binding although not in writing, even though by A's delay the carriage is not finished within a year. The object of this provision is to secure good evidence of contracts that will endure for a year's time or more.

It has been the common experience of man that the memories of people fail in a very short time. Even where they honestly try to state the exact terms of a contract it is difficult to do so after the lapse of a year or more.

"TO ANSWER FOR THE DEBT, DEFAULT, OR MIS-CARRIAGE OF ANOTHER."—If A promises to pay B's debt, he must make his promise in writing in accordance with the statute of frauds, or he can not be bound by the contract; but if A goes into a store with B and tells the storekeeper to let B have certain goods and that he, A, will pay for them, this is a different matter. It is an original promise by A himself, and the debt is not B's, but A's, and he will be obliged to pay, even though he

4

does not make the promise in writing. This promise must be made, however, to the creditor, and not to the debtor.

If A agrees with B for a consideration that he, A, will pay B's debts, B may compel A to do so, even though the agreement was not in writing.

"IN CONSIDERATION OF MARRIAGE EXCEPT MUTUAL PROMISES TO MARRY."—This provision has reference particularly to what are known as marriage settlements; as, where a man promises to deed a house and lot to a woman if she will marry him; or where a father promises his daughter $1,000 if she will marry. All such agreements must be in writing, or they are invalid. One exception is made of mutual promises. If one promises to marry another and does not fulfil his promise, even though it be an oral promise, which is usually the case, the party injured may recover damages.

"SALE OF PERSONAL PROPERTY."—If the price is uncertain at the time the contract is made, but subsequently proves to be more than $200, it can not be enforced, unless in writing; as, if a stack of hay is sold unmeasured at the rate of $5.00 per ton, and afterwards is found to contain fifty tons, the contract is invalid unless in writing. Whether acceptance of a sample will satisfy the statute depends on whether the sample is a mere specimen, or whether it is to constitute part of the thing sold. If the latter, it is sufficient to make valid an oral contract, even though the price is more than $200, but if a mere specimen, it is not considered as part of the thing sold.

PART PAYMENT must be "at the time" of the sale, and "payment" means actual payment in money, or its equivalent, not a mere credit. If the sale is made by auction, the auctioneer's memorandum must be made at the time of the sale. The auctioneer's clerk may make the memorandum.

LEASES AND SALES OF LAND.—Transactions regarding land have always been deemed important, and, as we shall see in a subsequent chapter, instruments affecting the title to real property must be placed on record with the recorder of the County in which the land is situated. Long verbal leases of land would tend to confusion in titles, and invite litigation. So in the sale of land, in all cases, a written instrument called a deed must be given from the seller to the buyer before there is any valid sale.

SUBDIVISION SEVEN, requiring an agent to be authorized in writing, to buy or sell real estate, is in harmony with the provisions of subdivisions five and six. If a principal can not make a valid sale of real estate without a writing, neither should his agent be allowed to do so.

TEST QUESTIONS.

1. Discuss the effect of the Statute of Frauds upon a sale by sample.
2. A and B enter into an agreement for the sale of goods. There is no evidence of the contract except that the day after the conversation A pays B $50 on account. Supposing the total price to be $500, will this payment satisfy the Statute so as to dispense with a writing?

CHAPTER X.

DEFENSES—STATUTE OF LIMITATIONS.

EXPLANATION.—It has been found by long experience that justice and right require that all suits at law for breach of contract should be brought within a reasonable time after the right accrues. If long delays are had, witnesses may be dead or their memories have failed, or in cases of written documents to be used as evidence, they may have been lost, and consequently great difficulty be had in proving the terms of the contract. It is right that a person charged with breach of contract should be afforded an opportunity to defend himself while he still may have evidence on hand with which to do so. It would be unfair to him if the party who claimed to be injured were allowed to wait for years, and then sue him, and compel him unjustly to pay money, or otherwise comply with the terms of an ancient contract.

Under the common law system no definite limits were fixed within which acts must be done, or contracts enforced, but merely a reasonable time was allowed. This, of course, led to a great deal of litigation to enable people to find out in each case what a reasonable time was; so that our modern statutes have in many cases fixed definitely the periods within which certain acts must be done, or suits brought.

These statutes are known under the general term of "Statute of Limitations." When the time has passed within which an action should have been brought, without its having been brought, the claim is said to be barred by the "Statute of Limitations," or, as it is more commonly called, "outlawed."

PROVISIONS.—The following are the principal periods of

(52)

limitation. *After ten years*, the State can not sue for the recovery of real estate claimed by, and in possession of, private persons.

After five years, an individual can not sue for the recovery of real property claimed by, and in the possession of, private persons.

After four years, an action can not be brought upon any contract, obligation, or liability founded upon an instrument in writing, executed in this State. Promissory notes and mortgages come under this head.

After three years, an action can not be maintained for

(1) Trespass upon real property;

(2) Taking, detaining, or injuring personal property;

(3) Relief on the ground of fraud or mistake.

After two years, an action can not be brought on oral contracts; or on contracts in writing, executed out of the State.

After one year, no action can be maintained for libel, slander, assault, battery, and false imprisonment.

After six months, an action can not be maintained against an officer to recover property or taxes illegally collected, nor against a county on claims which have been rejected.

In addition to the limitations prescribed for the commencement of actions, a lease of land is invalid if given for a longer period than *ten years*, and a lease of city lots if given for a longer period than *twenty years*.

OUTLAWED IN OTHER STATES.—Where a cause of action has arisen in another State or country, it is considered barred in every other State, without regard to the time of the limitation; thus, if a note became due and payable in Florida, and by the laws of that State became outlawed in two months, the note would also be outlawed in California, even though the Statutes of California prescribed four years as the time of limitation.

NO LIMITATION IN FAVOR OF BANKS.—There is no limitation to an action brought to recover money or other property deposited with any bank, trust company, or savings and loan society.

BEGINNING OF THE PERIOD.—Generally speaking, the Statute of Limitations begins to "run" whenever an action could be legally commenced; as, in case of a note, it begins the day after the note is due. In case of a current account, each item outlaws by itself as it is due, unless time is given, when the entire account outlaws from the end of the time.

In mutual accounts, that is, where goods are purchased by both parties, the time begins to run from the date of the last item on either side.

All store accounts, although they are entered in writing in books, are considered as oral contracts, and outlaw in two years.

In actions on the ground of fraud or mistake, the time begins to run from the time of the *discovery* by the aggrieved party of the facts constituting the fraud, and not from the time of the *commission* of the fraud, or *happening* of the mistake.

In case of a note payable on demand, the Statute begins to run from the date of the note, and not from the date of the demand.

DISABILITY OF CREDITOR.—If a person who is entitled to bring an action, be at the time the cause of action accrues, either,

(1) A minor;

(2) Insane;

(3) Imprisoned for a term less than life;

such person is said to be under disability, and the time during which such disability exists is not a part of the time limited for the commencement of the action; therefore, in case of a note being given in favor of a minor, it would not be outlawed until at least four years after the minor became of age, whether it was due before that time or not.

It must be remembered that the disability must have existed at the time the right to sue accrued.

When the Statute has commenced to run, subsequent disability will not stop it; thus, if the Statute has begun to run against a creditor on a note, and he becomes insane, and continues hopelessly insane, the Statute nevertheless will run, and the note will be outlawed in four years' time, without any allowance for the disability.

DEFENDANT OUT OF THE STATE.—If when the cause of action accrues against a person he is out of the State, or if after the cause of action accrues he goes out of the State, all of the time or times when he is actually out of the State are to be excluded from the time limited for the commencement of the action; thus, if a man leaves the State after the cause of action accrues on a note, and is gone six months, then returns and again goes for six months, the two absences are to be added together and the time of limitation is extended for the period of one year, hence in such a case there would in reality be five years before the note would be outlawed instead of four.

It has been held that a foreign corporation, such as an English Insurance Company having its agent in the State, is not absent from the State within the meaning of the Statute.

NEW PROMISES.—At the Common Law it was the rule that after a debt was barred by the Statute of Limitations, a new promise to pay, whether oral or written, would be sufficient to revive the debt.

This has been changed by Statute so that no acknowledgment or promise is sufficient evidence of a new or continuing contract by which to revive the debt, unless the same is contained in some writing, signed by the party to be charged thereby, and this written acknowledgment or promise must be direct, unequivocal, and unconditional, and made to the creditor.

An admission or promise to a stranger is not sufficient, and in case of joint debtors the promise of one does not avail against another. This new promise itself, being in writing, will be outlawed four years after the making of the promise.

PART PAYMENT is not sufficient in itself to revive a debt which has been barred by the Statute, unless it is evidenced by a writing signed by the debtor.

It is not sufficient that the *creditor* signs a writing or makes an endorsement upon a note, or otherwise executes a writing showing the payment. It must be done by the *debtor* or his agent.

IN CASE OF SUIT BROUGHT after a claim is outlawed, the person who wishes to rely on the fact of its being outlawed, must set up this fact and prove it in Court.

When this is done the Statute of Limitations is a good defense to the suit, and he is not obliged to carry out the contract.

TEST QUESTIONS.

1. An account is contracted February 1, 1894, for $100. On March 1, 1898, $50 is paid. May the payment of the remaining $50 be enforced?
2. A note is dated May 1, 1878; payment conditioned one day after date. It is not delivered till July 15, 1879. When is it barred by the Statute?
3. A man signs a note in Stockton, January 1, 1897, payable one year after date. Six months after he signs it he goes to Europe and remains five years. On what date will the note be outlawed?
4. A gave a note July 1, 1896; July 1, 1897, he became hopelessly insane. When will the note be outlawed?

CHAPTER XI.

DEFENSES—PERFORMANCE.

DEFINITION.—Performance is the carrying out of the contract in substantial accord with its terms. When this is done, the party so performing has a perfect defense against a suit brought against him for non-performance. This defense differs somewhat from that of the Statute of Limitations and the Statute of Frauds, in that while they are excuses for non-performance, in this defense the defendant simply says that he has performed the contract, and because of having performed it, he should not be compelled to perform his part of the contract a second time.

MANNER OF PERFORMANCE.—In order that a person may make good his defense of performance, he must show that he has performed his part of the contract in at least a substantial accordance with its terms.

It is not absolutely necessary that he should comply with every minute detail set forth in the contract as to the manner of performance, unless those details concern material parts.   .

Even if the contract prescribes a certain manner of performance, a debtor is excused from performing in that manner if his creditor gives him different directions in regard to the performance of his obligation; and if he performs the obligation in accordance with the later instructions of his creditor, the obligation is extinguished by such performance, even though the creditor does not receive the benefit of such performance.

As, if the agreement is that the debtor is to send certain money at a certain time by bank draft, and his creditor instructs him to send the money by express, the obligation is performed if he sends

(57)

it by express, even though the money be lost en route. A part performance of an obligation extinguishes the obligation to the extent of the part performance, if the contract is a divisible contract, but a part performance does not extinguish the obligation where the contract is indivisible; as, where a man agrees to build a dam before high water comes. He builds part of the dam and abandons the work. The high water comes and destroys the work he has done. The contract is indivisible. The part performance was of no value, and hence does not extinguish any part of the obligation.

TIME OF PERFORMANCE.—In most contracts time is not considered as being of the essence of the contract; that is, that it is not so important that the act must be done at the exact time specified in order to make the performance valid.

Unless a person can show that material damage has been suffered by reason of a contract's not being performed at a particular time, the performance will be good, even if not done at the exact time specified in the contract.

If a contract is to be performed within a certain time after date, the day of the date is excluded, and all of the last day which completes the time is included.

If the last day of performance or the particular day specified for performance falls on Sunday or a holiday, the act may be done on the next business day thereafter; as, if the day of performance fell on Sunday and Monday following was Washington's birthday, the next day, Tuesday, would be allowed for the performance. If no time is specified for the performance of an act a reasonable time is allowed. If the act is, in its nature, capable of being done instantly—as, for example, if it consists in the payment of money only—it must be performed immediately after the thing to be done is ascertained.

PLACE OF PERFORMANCE.—When the agreement specifies a particular place at which performance must be had, the performance should be had at that place, although if the performance is accepted at any other place, or can be had at any other place without material damage being done, it will nevertheless be a good performance; as, where a sum of money is to be paid at a certain bank, it should be paid at that bank, but if the creditor accepts payment of the money at any other place, he can not afterwards complain that the money was not paid at the bank, for the performance has been had without any damage to him.

PAYMENT.—The word "payment" is excluded in the term "performance," and means the performance of a contract for the delivery of money (which includes any kind of stamped metal or paper authorized by the government to circulate). The delivery of anything other than money is not payment; hence where a person owes money and gives a promissory note it is not payment in any sense, but simply an extension of the time within which to pay.

HOW PAYMENT APPLIED.—It sometimes happens that a debtor owes a certain creditor different sums of money upon different contracts; thus, he may owe a simple account, a promissory note, unsecured; and a promissory note secured by mortgage, to the same man. In such a case if he should pay his creditor $100 the question would arise, Which of the three debts should the hundred dollars be applied upon?

The rule is as follows:

(1) It must be applied to whichever debt the debtor directs it to be applied upon.

(2) If the debtor fails to make such directions the creditor may apply the payment as he pleases towards the extinction of any obligation, even though the obligation is outlawed at the time of the payment.

(3) If neither party make application within a reasonable time, such payments must be applied in the following order:

    I.—On interest;

    II.—On principal;

    III.—On the obligation earliest in maturity;

IV.—On an unsecured note;

V.—On a secured note.

EVIDENCE OF PAYMENT.—The ordinary evidence of the payment of a debt is a written receipt, signed by the creditor, stating in effect that the money has been paid.

This is good evidence of payment, but it is not always conclusive, as it may be possible that a receipt has been given by mistake or obtained through fraud, menace, duress, or undue influence; and a creditor may show any of these facts, if they be facts. So when an obligation has been delivered up to a debtor, such as a promissory note or mortgage, it is presumed that he has paid everything under it, though, of course, the contrary may be shown; so in case a person has a receipt for a later installment of money paid, it is presumed that he has paid all former installments; but in this case, as in the others, it may be shown that as a matter of fact he has not paid former installments.

GOOD TENDER is the offer of something in satisfaction of an obligation made in accordance with the terms of the contract, and with the intent to extinguish the obligation.

This, as a matter of defense to a suit, amounts to the same as actual performance. If a person can show that he has offered to perform in a proper manner, and the offer has been refused, he is not to suffer damage because he has not actually performed.

Good tender does not relieve a person from the obligation of performance, but it does relieve him from the consequences of failure of performance. He must hold himself ready to perform the obligation at all reasonable times thereafter, unless the performance should, by lapse of time, become impossible, as in case where the agreement was that A should deliver a certain horse, and the horse died after the time tender was made and acceptance was refused, further tender of performance was excused.

ESSENTIALS OF GOOD TENDER.—

(1) It must be in strict accordance with the terms of the contract; as in case the contract requires gold coin, it is necessary that

gold coin should be offered in payment. An offer of silver coin of equal amount would not be good tender.

(2) A tender in full is necessary. A tender of part of the amount of a debt is of no effect whatever as good tender.

(3) Tender must be made by the debtor or his agent. Tender by a stranger is not good tender.

· (4) It must be made at proper time. A tender of a load of wool at 11 o'clock at night was held to be bad tender, all warehouses being closed at that hour.

(5) To a proper person; that is, to a creditor or his agent.

(6) The place, if no place is specified in the contract, may be any place where the creditor may be found.

(7) The offer must be free from any condition, which the creditor is not bound on his part to perform. The creditor is always bound, however, to give a receipt for payment.

In case of payment of money, only such money as is authorized by the government for the payment of debts need be accepted, and the offer of any other kind of money is not good tender.

EFFECT OF GOOD TENDER.—When a person has made a good tender, and it is not accepted, this does not at once relieve him from the performance of the obligation at any subsequent time, but it does relieve him from the payment of interest, or any additional burdens which might accumulate after the tender was made; and it relieves him from any judgment for costs or expenses above the amount he has tendered, in case suit is brought against him.

If he makes the tender at the proper time, and it is refused, he must still be ready to perform his part of the contract at any time, or, in other words, he must keep his tender good, and in case he is sued he must show in his defense that he has made a good tender, and has continued to make the good tender.

He is not obliged, however, to hold his tender good forever. The Statute of Limitations will run against the claim, whatever it may be, and it will be outlawed whenever the limitation expires.

In tender of money the offer must be not only in the kind of money prescribed by the contract, but it must also be the exact amount. No one is required to give change. The matter of making change is only a matter of convenience, an accommodation which a creditor is usually willing to grant to his debtor, but if the creditor demands the exact amount, it is not a good tender to tender a greater amount and demand change.

ACCORD AND SATISFACTION.—Under some circumstances, a creditor will find it to his advantage to accept part payment of his debt and give a receipt in full rather than to insist on a payment in full. If it is money that is to be paid, the debtor may not have any money and the creditor may be willing to accept as full payment something altogether different; as, a horse.

In such a case, an agreement to accept something less or different from that specified in the contract as full performance, is called an "accord," and when the agreement is carried out, and the acceptance is actually had, this is called "satisfaction;" e. g., A owes B $100; B agrees to accept $90 in full payment. This is an accord. A pays the $90, and gets a receipt in full. This is satisfaction. The transaction would be in legal effect the same if A had offered and B had accepted a horse instead of the $100. It makes no difference whether there has been a dispute as to the correct amount of the bill or not. It is nevertheless an "accord and satisfaction" when the conditions of the definition are fulfilled.

The contract of accord and satisfaction is an exception to the ordinary rule of contracts, in that no new consideration is required, and when satisfaction is had under an accord, the creditor can not afterwards collect the remainder of the debt.

In order that accord and satisfaction may be used as a defense to a suit it is, of course, necessary that a defendant in his answer to a suit should show that the accord had been entered into, and that satisfaction had been had.

Accord without satisfaction is not a bar to an action. The plaintiff must show that the accord has been executed.

ARBITRATION AND AWARD.—Courts have been instituted as means of settling disputes between individuals in regard to business transactions, and Courts are most frequently resorted to when one of the parties is unwilling to settle at all, and where the object is to compel him to settle. It sometimes happens, however, that both parties are willing to settle the matter but are unable to agree as to the proper settlement, and yet do not wish to maintain a lawsuit. In such a case they may agree to leave the decision of the case to third parties, and agree that they will abide by their decision. It is customary for one to select an arbitrator, the other to select another, and the two arbitrators to select a third. The three thus chosen are called a Board of Arbitration. The Board of Arbitrators will examine into the disputed matter and render a decision in favor of one party or the other, and if this decision is properly made on a full understanding of the facts, it is binding upon both parties, and neither one can afterwards maintain a suit at law against the other in the same matter for an amount larger than the amount allowed by the Board of Arbitration. The decision thus given by the Board of Arbitration is called "award."

The agreement to submit to arbitration is not a binding agreement, however, as either party may revoke his consent to the arbitration at any time before the award is actually made.

LIS PENDENS.— This is a Latin phrase meaning "a suit pending." It would be harassing and vexatious if a man were allowed to bring two suits against his debtor upon the same cause of action, in the same Court, at the same time; and it is against the policy of the law to permit a multiplicity of suits; hence a person can not bring two suits at the same time against the same person, upon the same cause of action, for the same relief, in the same Court.

If all these essentials are not present, a person can not claim that another suit is pending.

When they are all present, the claim of *lis pendens* is a valid defense to a second suit brought against a defendant.

Thus, if A sued B upon a certain note for $500, B could say that there was a suit pending if A again sued on the same $500 before the first suit had been disposed of, while it would be perfectly proper for A to sue B for the amount of $500, and at the same time sue him for damages for breach of a different contract.

COUNTER CLAIM.—It sometimes happens that when a debtor owes his creditor, the creditor may also owe the debtor an amount, so that when a suit is brought the defendant may present his claim against the plaintiff, and this counter claim must be subtracted from the original amount of the debt; or if it is an amount equal to the debt sued for it will be a full defense, an equal set-off against the plaintiffs claim; for example, if A is sued by B on a claim of $100 for breach of contract, A, if he has one, may set up in his answer a counter claim for $50, if it be a claim also arising on contract, but a claim for injuries could not be set up as a counter claim to a claim arising upon contract; and the claim must· exist in favor of the defendant against the plaintiff.

A claim set up by a third party is not good as a counter claim, neither can a claim which is barred by the Statute of Limitations be set up as a counter claim.

If the defendant fails to set up a counter claim in his answer, he can not afterwards bring a separate suit for the amount.

The reason of this doctrine of counter claim is to prevent a multiplicity of suits by compelling parties to test the validity of their claims in a single action.

TEST QUESTIONS.

1. A contracts to build a large court-house in a day. Is he answerable in damages for failure to fulfil his contract?

2. A agreed to pay a debt in salt to be packed in barrels, to be furnished by the creditor. The creditor did not furnish the barrels. Would that excuse A from delivering the salt?
3. Distinguish between "legal" tender and "good" tender.
4. A owes B $100, but is unable to pay it. He offers B a wagon in satisfaction of the debt, which B accepts. What is the legal term for the transaction?

CHAPTER XII.

NEGOTIABLE PAPER.

NEGOTIABLE PAPER can not be well explained in a single brief definition. It has been used as a medium of exchange and as evidence of debt for many hundreds of years. It is an exception to the general rule of contracts in that its collection may be enforced by an innocent holder, even where fraud has been practised in obtaining it originally; and it also protects an innocent holder against other like defenses. The chief difference between negotiable paper and ordinary written contracts is that negotiable paper has the function of passing from hand to hand, as money, and can be collected by an innocent holder for value, while mere assignable paper is charged with all equities between the original parties.

It must be thoroughly understood before we can fully understand what a negotiable instrument is, that it is the rule of contracts that certain contracts can not be transferred from one to another, and even when written contracts are of such a nature that they may be transferred from one person to another generally, still the person who accepts the transfer from a person who has not a good title himself, does not get any better title than the seller had.

Suppose that A had stolen a horse; he, of course, has no good title to the horse; he sells the horse to B. No matter how much B may have paid for the horse, nor how innocent of wrongdoing he may have been, he gets no good title to the horse, the thief having none.

In the case of negotiable paper, however, if A had stolen a

(66)

negotiable note instead of the horse, and sold it to B, B, being an innocent purchaser, before maturity of the note, B then would have had a perfectly good title to the note, and could collect it from the maker.

This distinction will be fully discussed later.

THE ESSENTIALS of every negotiable instrument are:

(1) In writing;

(2) An unconditional promise or request;

(3) Negotiable in form;

(4) Payable in money only;

(5) For a definite sum payable generally;

(6) To an ascertained and designated payee;

(7) Time for payment must be certain;

(8) Properly signed.

It must be carefully borne in mind that the above are absolutely essential to negotiable paper. Any paper which lacks any of these elements is not a negotiable instrument.

IN WRITING includes writing in script, with pen or pencil, printing, typewriting, or any method of placing thoughts upon an impressible substance; or it may be partly in handwriting, partly printed, or partly typewritten. The rule is the same in this regard as in ordinary contracts.

SIGNATURE.—A signature is usually and properly the name of the person who executes the instrument, written by himself at the bottom of the instrument, with the intention of signing it, but anything written anywhere on a negotiable instrument may be proved as a signature. A signature stamped upon a note with a rubber stamp has been held good, and even in one case where a person wrote the figures "128" on the back of a note, pretending to the payee, who could not read, that it was his proper signature, the Court held that the figures so written were the signature of the person making them.

NEGOTIABLE IN FORM.—The words "to order" or "to bearer" are the customary words showing negotiability. They indicate that it is permitted to transfer the note from one person to another. These words, or some equivalent words, such as "pay to any one," or "pay to myself or order," renders an instrument negotiable in form. Without some such words the instrument is not negotiable.

Where a person makes a note payable to an obviously fictitious payee, such as "pay to Robinson Crusoe," it is equivalent to "pay to bearer."

PAYABLE IN MONEY ONLY.—Money is the standard by which we measure the value of all other articles, and being a standard it is presumed to be an invariable standard; that is to say, $100 to-day is presumed to be worth just $100 at any future time; hence the certainty of receiving the amount stipulated for by a note in passing from hand to hand is only obtained by making it payable in money only.

If it were payable in wheat, the price of which is constantly fluctuating, no one but a mere speculator would care to take such an instrument to hold for any certain time. Money therefore being the only convenient imperishable standard measure of values, is the only thing which can serve as a basis for commercial paper.

AN UNCONDITIONAL PROMISE OR REQUEST.—If the promise made is a conditional one, it would, of course, render the payment uncertain, and thus be open to the same objection as would the instrument if made payable in commodities instead of money; thus a promise to pay "if a sale be made in twelve months," or a promise to pay "when convenient," renders the paper non-negotiable.

A DEFINITE SUM.—A promise to pay "a reasonable attorney's fee," is uncertain, and renders a note not negotiable, while a promise to pay "$50 attorney's fee" does not affect negotiability.

The law has drawn some fine distinctions, however, in these matters, and it has been held that "payable with exchange," does not affect negotiability, because exchange can always be determined without difficulty.

This is under the maxim, "That is certain which can be made certain."

PAYABLE GENERALLY, means payable out of general funds, and not out of specific funds, as "payable out of funds now on deposit in the Farmers Bank" would render the note not negotiable as being out of a specific fund. No one could tell at the time of receiving the note whether the money was still on deposit in the Farmers Bank.

ASCERTAINED AND DESIGNATED PAYEE.—The following designations have been held sufficient,—"Pay to bills payable" equals "to bearer," "Pay to trustees acting under the will of A," "Pay to A or his heirs," "Pay to John Doe," equals, "Pay to bearer," "Pay to the now secretary of a certain corporation," it being held that in all of the above cases that while the designation made does not specify definitely a certain person, yet the designation is sufficiently accurate so that the payee may be found, and under the maxim, "That is certain which can be made certain," the designations have been held good.

Where a note was made payable "to the secretary" of a certain corporation, it was held not to be sufficiently certain as a designation of the person, as the corporation might change its secretary at any time.

If no payee be named at all the instrument is mere waste paper; as for example, "Pay on the within $750."

TIME CERTAIN.—A negotiable instrument may be with or without date, with or without designation of the time or place of payment, but if it does not specify the time of payment, it is payable immediately, and when it does specify a time, it is absolutely necessary that the time specified should be certain or be capable of being made certain; as, if payable on demand, or at sight, the time can be made certain.

An instrument payable "when I am of age," is uncertain, as there is no certainty of the maker's reaching his majority.

If a negotiable instrument falls due on Sunday, or other holiday, it is payable on the next business day thereafter, the time being extended by reason of the holiday.

Days of grace are three days which were allowed to a debtor for payment of his obligation after the time of its maturity.

These days of grace are not now allowed.

GENERALLY.—The amount stated in negotiable instruments should be written both in words and figures. Where there is a difference between the words and figures, the amount written in words controls.

A negotiable instrument may contain a pledge of collateral security with authority to dispose thereof, but it must not contain any other contract further than this.

A due bill, such as is often given as an acknowledgment of a debt, is not in any sense a negotiable instrument, being a mere acknowledgment that money is due, and not being a promise of payment.

The words "for value received," often seen in a negotiable instrument, are useless. The law presumes that a written instrument has been given for value. These presumptions may, of course, be rebutted, and this would be so whether the words "for value received" were inserted or not.

There are six different classes of negotiable instruments, viz.:

(1) Bills of Exchange;

(2) Promissory Notes;

(3) Bank Notes;

(4) Checks;

(5) Bonds; and

(6) Certificates of Deposit.

FRAUD, MISTAKE, DURESS.—If a person procures another to sign a negotiable instrument through either fraud, mistake, or duress, it can not be collected by the person committing such fraud, or guilty of such duress, or participating in the mistake; but should such person sell the instrument before maturity to an innocent purchaser in the usual course of business, who paid value for it, that person would have a right to collect the note from the maker, notwithstanding such irregularity in the making of the instrument. So, also, as before explained, if an owner loses a negotiable instrument, the finder has no title and can not collect it from the maker, but if the finder sells it to an innocent purchaser before maturity, that purchaser has an absolute right to collect from the maker.

This is the distinguishing characteristic of the contract entered into by one who signs a negotiable instrument, and wherein such contracts differ from all other contracts.

Of course, a person whose name has been forged to a negotiable paper, can not be compelled to pay it no matter who holds it, or how innocent the holder may be of any wrongdoing, because he has not signed the instrument and it is not his instrument.

TEST QUESTIONS.

1. Is the following negotiable? Give reasons.

December 1, 1896.

On demand I promise to pay to R. S. Cox One hundred ($100) dollars with interest at Ten (10) per cent per annum.

R. Boyd.

2. A made out a note payable "to bearer" and left it lying on his desk. His clerk stole the note and sold it to B, who did not know it to be stolen. Can B compel A to pay the note at maturity? Give reasons.

3. Suppose in the above case A had signed the note, but left the amount blank. Can B compel A to pay it at maturity?

CHAPTER XIII.

PROMISSORY NOTES.

DEFINITION.—A Promissory Note is an unconditional promise in writing by a person to pay a certain sum of money, generally, "to bearer," or "to order," of some one named therein, at a specified time.

A promissory note is merely given as evidence of a debt. In legal effect it is not a debt in itself, and when we say a person owes another a note, in strictness we mean that he owes a sum of money and that the debt is evidenced by the note.

It is in that respect merely a means of proof that one man owes another money, but it is also more than this in that under certain rules and conditions governing negotiable paper, a promissory note may circulate as money and may have a certain value in the markets of the business world.

If no time is specified for the payment of a note, it is due at once. If no place is specified for the payment of a note, it is payable at the place of residence or business of the maker, or at any place where he may be found.

FORM.—In regard to the form of promissory notes, it is possible to have a great variety. One form is as good as another, so far as negotiability is concerned, provided it contains all the elements required as specified under the general head of "Negotiable Paper."

The ordinary form is as follows:—

$100.00

                                  Stockton, Cal., Jan. 2, 1898.

Six (6) months after date I promise to pay J. Boyd, or order, One hundred ($100.00) Dollars.

(72)   M. Meyers.

In addition, there may be inserted in the above outline any or all of the following clauses after the word "Dollars;" "together with interest at the rate of six (6) per cent per annum, payable semiannually, and if not so paid when due to be added to the principal and become a part thereof, and bear interest at the same rate;" also, "I agree to pay in case suit or action is instituted to collect this note, or any part thereof, the sum of Twenty ($20) Dollars as attorney's fee in such suit or action;" "and further, I herewith pledge my gold watch, No. 7421, as security for the payment of this note, and hereby authorize J. Boyd to dispose of said watch and apply the proceeds to the payment of this note, in case I fail to pay said note at its maturity."

If two persons wish to make a note so that both will be liable to pay it, they usually write "WE promise to pay, etc.," in which case it is called a *joint note;* or it may read, "We or either of us promise to pay, etc.," in which case it is called a *joint and several note.*

In either case, however, the makers are individually and jointly liable to pay the full amount of the note.

The note may provide for the payment in installments, and for any rate of interest, payable at any specified times. It may be payable on demand, or at a certain date, or after a certain date. It may be written and signed on paper or any substitute, in any language, in pencil or in ink.

PARTIES.—The original parties to a note are termed the *maker,* the person whose name is signed as promisor, and the *payee,* the person to whom the promise is given.

If the payee writes his name on the back of the instrument with the intent to transfer it to a third party, he is then called an endorser, and the person to whom he transfers it is an endorsee, and in like manner when this endorsee transfers it and writes his name on the back thereof, he becomes an endorser, and the person to whom he transfers the note, the endorsee, and so on as often as it is transferred.

NEGOTIABILITY.—It must be carefully remembered and thoroughly understood that in order to be negotiable, a note must contain all the elements required to constitue a negotiable instrument.

A person may give a written contract for the payment of money, and while it may be in form somewhat like a promissory note, if it lacks any one of the essentials it is not a negotiable instrument; hence the utmost care must be taken not to confuse instruments which are often passed as promissory notes with negotiable instruments proper; and it is important to remember that while a mere written contract for the payment of money can be transferred by endorsement, and may pass from one hand to another, it is nevertheless a mere written contract, and a holder gets no more rights under it than he does under any ordinary contract, and he accepts it subject to any defenses which may be made between the original parties.

CONSIDERATION.—As we have seen, it is one of the rules of contracts that every contract must have a sufficient consideration, and this is also the rule in negotiable instruments, so far as the original parties are concerned; but even if A signs a note without any consideration, and an innocent holder, for value, before maturity, presents it for payment at maturity, A can not refuse to pay on the ground of want of consideration, it being the peculiar characteristic of negotiable paper that an innocent holder must be protected.

Therefore, so far as innocent holders are concerned, promissory notes are an exception to the rule that a consideration is required.

ACCOMMODATION NOTE.—A wishes to borrow money, but has no security to offer. B is a friend of A, who has no money, but has property. He signs a note payable to A, which A takes to the bank and borrows money upon. A, of course, expects to pay the note at maturity, but if he does not, the bank can compel B to pay the note, notwithstanding the fact that it was given without consideration. All of the parties knew that the note was given without consideration, and for the purpose specified. Such a note is called an Accommodation Note, and by the laws of business, does not require consideration. A, however, should he play false to his friend, could not collect the money on the note from B, though the bank could.

Of course, in an accommodation note it is not necessary that any purchaser be innocent in order that he may collect from the maker. In fact, he usually knows that no consideration has passed.

BONA FIDE HOLDER.—A person who receives without notice of irregularities, a negotiable promissory note, in the usual course of business, for value, before maturity, is called a bona-fide holder, and such a person has an absolute right to collect the amount due on the note at maturity from the maker; but if such a holder sells the note, and afterwards it is given back to him, he does not thereby retake the absolute right of collection, but takes it as a gift subject to all equities and defenses between the original parties; so a finder or a thief can not collect a note, but his bona-fide endorsee may collect it. *An equitable defense* is one which does not appear on the face of the note, and which does not destroy its negotiability as fraud, force, theft, incapacity, payment; and even of these defenses, a maker can only avail himself when they are between him and his payee.

FORGERY may be committed either by signing another's name to a note, or by a material alteration in the note.

No one, as we have before observed, acquires any rights under a forged name, neither does he acquire any rights where an alteration has been made, unless the alteration has been made possible through the negligence of the maker; as, where he writes in lead-pencil, or leaves blanks which may be easily filled; but in any event the alteration must be material.

The following are material alterations:

(1) Change of date of note;

(2) Change in time of payment;

(3) Change in amount or interest;

(4) Change from "gold" to "silver," or "pounds" to "dollars;"

(5) Change in parties;

(6) Change in liability of parties; as where a maker's name is changed so as to make him liable only as surety;

(7) Change in place of payment.

BANK BILLS are promissory notes issued by a bank. A private bank has no authority to issue notes to circulate as money.

National banks, however, are allowed to issue notes secured by deposit of Government Bonds in the United States Treasury, and these notes circulate as money without the necessity of endorsement, being made payable "to bearer," and being practically guaranteed by the United States Government.

Such notes are in a sense negotiable after having been paid by the maker, as they can be immediately passed out again as money, and preserve their negotiability when thus sent forth.

BONDS.—A Bond is in legal effect identical with a promissory note; in fact, it is a promise to pay money, usually of large denominations, and is a very formal document, having attached to it separate promises called coupons, to pay the interest on the Bond.

Bonds are most frequently issued by some branch of the governmental authority, state, county, district, or nation, and their payment is in such case provided for by taxation.

They are signed by the executive officers of the governing body of the municipality which issues them, and are negotiable to the same extent and for the same purpose as an ordinary promissory note.

TEST QUESTIONS.

1. Is the following negotiable? Give reasons.

I promise to pay to S. Brown, or order, within six months from date, the sum of Fifty ($50.00) Dollars, and in case suit is brought for the collection of this note I promise to pay a reasonable attorney's fee.

J. Gould.

2. A is a merchant; B comes to him after banking hours; shows him a note for $100, apparently signed by a responsible party, due thirty days hence; says he is in urgent need of cash at once and will take $50 for the note. A buys the note from him for $50 and afterwards learns that the signature has been forged. What remedy, if any, has A?

3. Suppose in the above case the signature was genuine, but had been obtained by B through fraud. Could A collect the note from the maker? Give reasons.

4. A forger has "raised" a note from $40 to $140. Discuss the rights of collection by A, who is a subsequent holder.

CHAPTER XIV.

BILLS OF EXCHANGE.

EXPLANATION.—In the early days of commercial activity it was found inconvenient and unsafe for persons doing business at a distance to send the actual coin from one place to another, and there was invented and brought into use what are known as Bills of Exchange.

Suppose A in San Francisco transacts business with B in New York. A owes B $1,000. Instead of sending the coin he goes to the San Francisco Bank, pays in his thousand dollars, and gets a Bill of Exchange or draft drawn in favor of B against the New York Bank, and sends it by mail to B.

On receipt of this Bill of Exchange B goes to the New York Bank, endorses the bill, and is paid a thousand dollars. In each case the parties pay to the bank a small amount as compensation.

B or some other man in New York wishes to send money to pay a debt in San Francisco. He goes to the New York Bank, pays his money, receives a draft, sends it to San Francisco, and his creditor gets his money from the San Francisco Bank.

In this way the New York and San Francisco Banks keep even or nearly so on the amount of money owing the one to the other.

If at any time the balance in favor of the one or the other gets too large, and there seems no prospect of getting even otherwise than by sending the coin, the balance is shipped in the actual coin across the continent. This, however, rarely or never occurs.

These Bills of Exchange, or drafts, as they are usually called, if drawn between parties in the same state or country, may be

(78)

endorsed and passed from hand to hand as money and are subject to all the rules concerning promissory notes and negotiable paper in general, and being issued usually by banks generally have a higher commercial value than promissory notes.

DEFINITION.—A bill of exchange is an unconditional order or request in writing by one person to another directing the payment "to order" of a person named therein, or "to bearer," of a certain sum of money, generally at a certain time.

The following is the ordinary form of a Bill.

THE FARMERS' BANK.

No. 2140.   Stockton, Cal., Jan. 2d, 1898.

At sight pay to the order of Thomas Sawyer Five Hundred ($500.00) Dollars.

M. TWAIN,

To First National Bank,   Cashier.

Boston, Mass.

FOREIGN BILLS.—A Foreign Bill is one which is drawn in one country to be paid in another, or in one state to be paid in another. On account of the liability or possibility of a bill's being lost in transmission, it has been customary to draw the bill in duplicate or triplicate, and send the copies by different routes, especially when between different countries where mails are carried by ships; as between different states, bills are now seldom drawn even in duplicate.

A creditor, however, may demand, as a matter of right, under the law, that his debtor shall execute the bill of exchange in triplicate, each copy stating the existence of the others, and all forming one set.

INLAND BILL.—The Inland Bill is almost universally used as a means of paying debts between people in different parts of the same state or country. It is never drawn in sets. An Inland Bill is universally known as a draft.

PARTIES.—By examining the form above shown, it will be seen that there are three original parties. The one who signs the draft, M. Twain, is called the Drawer. The one to whom it is addressed, The First National Bank, Boston, Mass., and who is to pay the draft, is called the Drawee, and the one to whom it is made payable, Thomas Sawyer, is called the Payee.

Sometimes a person wishes to visit a distant city and not carry money on his person. He draws a draft in favor of himself. In such case he is both drawer and payee.

The subsequent parties are endorsees and endorsers, as in the case of promissory notes, and there may of course be any number of them.

TIME OF PAYMENT.—A draft such as the above is called a *Sight draft*, and means that it is to be paid as soon as the drawee sees it, or when it is presented to him for payment.

A draft payable "on demand" is practically a sight draft, and due upon presentation. A draft may be drawn any number of days after sight. In such cases it is called a time draft. The object of a time draft is either to accommodate the debtor and creditor in the transaction, who may have reasons for wishing to defer payment, or to accommodate the bank, if it is a large draft, in order that it may make provisions for its payment. Days of grace are not allowed on drafts.

ACCEPTANCE.—When a sight draft is presented to the drawee, the drawee must either pay it or refuse to do so. He is under no obligation to pay it and trust the drawer for his money, unless he chooses to do so.

In the case of a time draft, the payee should present it to the drawee for acceptance. Without this presentment, the drawee may not even know of the existence of the draft, and may not be prepared to pay it when due, so that it is customary and proper for the payee immediately upon the receipt of the draft, to take it to the drawee and notify him that he holds such an instrument.

The drawee, if he wishes to pay it when due, will "accept" the draft by writing the word "accepted" across the face of the draft with the date, and his name; or simply his name with or without date or other words, will be a binding acceptance, and is in effect his promise to pay the draft when due.

A draft payable ten days after sight would be due ten days after such acceptance. The acceptance, therefore, has the double object of making the drawee liable for its payment, and fixing the time, in case of a time draft, of its maturity.

If the drawee refuses to accept the draft he is said to "dishonor" it, and the draft is said to be "dishonored."

ACCEPTANCE FOR HONOR.—When a drawee dishonors a bill, it may have passed through a number of hands, and the dishonor of the bill cause considerable trouble to some or all of the parties thereto, hence it is a rule of law that after a bill has thus been dishonored it may be accepted or paid by any person for the honor of any party thereto.

The holder of the bill is not bound to let it be accepted for honor, but he is bound to accept payment for honor, if it is tendered.

The person who accepts or pays for honor, must write a statement on the bill showing for whose honor he accepts or pays, and must give notice to that party of the fact of such acceptance or payment within a reasonable time. Having done so he is entitled to reimbursement from him, and from all parties prior to him.

PRESENTMENT FOR ACCEPTANCE.—Drafts payable at sight, on demand, or after sight, must be presented within ten days plus a reasonable time for transmission to the place of presentment.

Delay in presentment for acceptance is excused, however, when caused by circumstances over which the holder has no control.

As to how presentment should be made, the following rules exist:

(1) The draft must be presented by the holder or his agent;

6

(2) On a business day within reasonable hours;

(3) To the drawee or his agent.

The drawee has until the next business day to accept or refuse the draft. If the drawee, or his agent, or place of business can not be found, the presentment is excused.

AS A NEGOTIABLE INSTRUMENT, a draft is identical with a promissory note, being subject to the same equities and defenses and endowing a bona-fide holder with the same rights and privileges. A bona-fide holder gets a good title without regard to whether he took the bill before acceptance or after, so long as he procures it before maturity.

LETTER OF CREDIT.—This is a form of non-negotiable draft which does not specify definitely any particular drawee, but is given generally on any bank or banker requesting them to pay the payee any sum or sums upon a certain amount stated in the letter.

This is for convenience of persons who are taking extensive tours. Instead of carrying money they take the letter of credit, having first deposited with their local bank a sum of money, and in each city with which the local bank does business, the traveler may present his letter of credit, and draw any amount not to exceed that specified in the letter, less the amount already drawn.

It is the duty of the bank from which he draws to write upon the letter the date of payment, the name of the bank so paying, and the amount paid.

The bank which pays the last amount, making the total called for in the letter, keeps the letter to be used as a voucher in settling with the other banks.

As each bank pays the traveler, it draws on the local bank for the amount, which it has paid, to reimburse itself.

Letters of credit, while they are used in a similar manner as negotiable instruments, and we classify them under that head, are usually not negotiable, being drawn in favor of one person only, whose signature is clearly identified.

TEST QUESTIONS.

1. Explain the transaction of sending $100 to a friend in New York by regular Bank Exchange.
2. A payee fails to present a draft for payment within the proper time after acceptance. The drawee becomes insolvent before payment. Discuss the liabilities of the parties.
3. A bill becomes due December 1st, 1896; December 5th, 1896, A purchases the bill in good faith and for a valuable consideration. Discuss A's rights and liabilities and. the rights and liabilities of the drawer.
4. On March 1st, 1897, A buys a negotiable instrument which is dated July 1st, 1896, payable six months after date. Discuss A's right to recover on the paper.

CHAPTER XV.

CHECKS.

DEFINITION.—A Check is a bill of exchange drawn upon a bank or banker against deposit funds, payable on demand, without grace, and without interest.

EXPLANATION.—The use of checks is much more recent than that of bills of exchange proper.

Checks are usually used only for making payments in a particular locality, town, or city. A business man who necessarily pays out large sums of money, obviates the necessity of making change, on paying his bills, and secures himself against robbers, by placing his money on deposit in a bank and drawing checks for the exact amount required to pay any bill presented.

The check when presented and paid at the bank is marked "paid" and a record is kept of such payment on the bank books, so that there is an additional receipt in case the creditor attempts to make a second collection.

Checks are sometimes made so that they do not conform to the requirements of negotiability. In such cases they amount to mere orders for the payment of money, and afford no protection whatever to a holder more than any ordinary written contract.

The following is the ordinary form of checks:

Stockton, Cal., January 2, 1898.   Number 10.

THE FARMERS' BANK.

Pay to R. M. Stanley, or order, One Hundred and $\frac{25}{100}$ ($100.25) Dollars.

L. M. McCOY.

(84)

PARTIES AND THEIR LIABILITIES.—The names of the parties are, of course, the same as in any other bill of exchange, and their liability is the same, except that the drawer and endorsers are exonerated by delay in presentment only to the extent of the injury which they suffer thereby; and further, an endorsee after its apparent maturity, but without actual notice of its dishonor, acquires a title equal to that of an endorsee before such period.

The drawer in executing the check agrees that there are funds on deposit in the bank for its payment, and that the bank will pay the amount upon proper presentment.

Sometimes a bank will even cash a check when the drawer has not actually coin on deposit with which to pay it, but in doing so the bank, of course, takes the chances on the maker's insolvency, or his refusing to deposit further with them. In any event the bank is not obliged to cash the check, and can not be compelled to do so even if the maker has funds on deposit, so that in case of refusal of payment the payee must seek his remedy against the maker, provided he has presented the check within proper time, and has given proper notice of the refusal of the bank to pay.

PRESENTMENT OF A CHECK FOR PAYMENT, as in the case of a bill of exchange proper, must be made within ten days after the time in which it can with reasonable diligence be transmitted to the proper place for such presentment, and if not presented, the drawer and endorsers are exonerated, unless such presentment is excused; and delay or failure of presentment is only excused when caused by circumstances over which the holder has no control.

Example.—A draws a check against The Farmers' Bank in favor of B. B uses reasonable diligence and it requires two days to reach the bank. The bank fails on the 11th day after the check is issued. The drawer is responsible for the payment of the check.

Suppose that B is immediately accessible to the bank, and does not go to the bank for the purpose of presentment until the 15th day. The bank fails on the 14th day. B must lose the money. The law gives him ten days after he reaches the bank within which to present his check. If he fails to do so, he must suffer for his own negligence. So far as A, the drawer, is concerned, the check is presumed to be paid after ten days plus the reasonable time required to reach the bank.

This rule is a very just one, otherwise in the above case A would be required to keep large sums of money on deposit to meet checks drawn an indefinite time beforehand, and be constantly liable to extra losses in case of the failure of the bank.

It is to be noted, however, that no matter how long a time elapses after the drawing of the check, the holder may cash it provided there is funds in the bank, and the bank is still doing business.

CERTIFIED CHECKS.—There is nothing to prevent a person who is so disposed from drawing a check upon a bank in which he has no funds deposited, and which he knows will not be cashed. This being true, a creditor before receiving a check in payment will often require that it be "certified," which means that the cashier of the bank against which it is drawn is to write the word "certified," or "good," or some equivalent word, with his name, across the face of the check.

This has the legal effect of making the bank responsible for the payment and is practically the same thing so far as fixing the liability of the bank, as the acceptance of a draft, except that in the case of acceptance of a draft, the drawer still remains liable, while in the case of certification of a check, the drawer is released and the bank only is liable.

The bank, after having certified a check, will always make note on the depositor's account, of the amount certified, charging him with the certification in a similar manner as if the money had been actually paid.

If there is no money on deposit, the bank will not certify the check, and the creditor will refuse to accept it.

The principal reason for having a check certified is that the bank is usually more reliable financially than an individual. An oral certification is of no effect. It must be written.

FORGERY.—A check is liable to forgery in the same manner as any other negotiable instrument, by the signing of another's name, or by alteration; and the question frequently arises in case of loss by forgery, whether the bank or the maker must bear the loss.

In forgery of signature the rule is that the bank must know the signature of its depositors.

When a person opens a deposit account with the bank, the bank should require him to write his signature in a book kept for that purpose, just as he expects to write it in drawing checks, and the bank is thereafter conclusively presumed to know the depositor's signature, and if it pays out any money on his account on a forged signature, no matter how cleverly it may be executed, the bank must stand the loss.

The rule, however, is different as regards forgery by alteration. If the drawer has properly and carefully filled all blanks with some indelible writing material, so that the checks can not be easily altered, the bank must stand the loss if the note is altered, and the bank pays a larger sum than that for which the check was originally drawn.

On the other hand, if by the drawer's ordinary carelessness in leaving blanks, or writing lightly, or with pencil, he renders the forgery easily consummated, the drawer must bear the loss.

The maxim of law upon which this rule rests is: "Of two innocent parties he must suffer who made the wrong possible."

BANK BOOK.—When a person deposits money in a bank against which he wishes to draw checks, he is given a small bank book ruled with debit and credit columns, for the purpose of keeping a record of money deposited and checked out.

When a deposit is made, the bank enters the amount on the left page, and this operates as a receipt.

Periodically the depositor hands his book to the cashier, and the amount of the checks drawn is entered on the other page and the book balanced, thus showing him at any given time just how much money is to his credit.

CERTIFICATE OF DEPOSIT.—If a person wishes to deposit money in a bank without any intention of drawing checks against the deposit, and simply for safe keeping, the bank will give him what is called a Certificate of Deposit.

The ordinary form is as follows:

THE FARMERS' BANK.

No. 560.

This certifies that J. Brown has deposited in this bank Five Hundred ($500.00) Dollars, payable to the order of himself on return of this Certificate properly endorsed.

R. EDWARDS,
Cashier.

It should be noticed that the words of negotiability are slightly different from those in other negotiable instruments. The word "promise" is not used, the word "payable" being substituted. It is, however, a negotiable instrument and may circulate from hand to hand indefinitely.

An ordinary check signed by the cashier of the bank is sometimes drawn in lieu of the Certificate of Deposit, and serves exactly the same purpose. It is called a cashier's check.

TEST QUESTIONS.

1. A person presents a check to a bank for payment. The bank pays the check and afterwards discovers that the signature is a forgery. Who loses the amount of the check?

2. September 1st, 1896, a Stockton grocer gives a check to a Stockton merchant for $100. September 14th, the merchant takes the check to the bank and finds that the bank has suspended payment. Can he compel the grocer to pay him another $100? Give reasons.

3. A check is forged by altering the amount stated therein from $100 to $200. The bank pays $200 on the check. Who must lose the $100, the bank or the maker? Discuss fully.

4 A draws a check on a bank December 1st, 1897; he gives it to B in payment of a debt December 15th, 1897. December 30th B goes to the bank and finds that the bank was insolvent December 10th. Can he compel the payment of the debt by A? Discuss fully.

CHAPTER XVI.

TRANSFER OF NEGOTIABLE PAPER.

BONA-FIDE HOLDER.—We have before stated that a bona-fide holder is one who takes a negotiable instrument,

(1) For value;

(2) Without notice of defects;

(3) In the usual course of business; and

(4) Before maturity.

FOR VALUE.—It is, as we have learned, the general rule of all contracts that there must be a valuable consideration, or the contract is void, and this rule holds good in regard to negotiable paper.

It is not necessary that actual money value be paid or that something equal in value be paid. The valuable consideration may be merely the forbearance to sue on an obligation; but in any event unless there is some substantial value given the transaction would give rise to suspicion of fraud.

This rule is a just one, for if a person has paid nothing for an instrument he loses nothing, and is not injured if the instrument is void.

WITHOUT NOTICE OF DEFECTS.—By defects in negotiable paper we mean that there has been fraud, duress, menace, mistake, want of consideration, or some such like irregularity between the original parties at the time the paper was executed.

In order that a person may claim to be a bona-fide holder and have all the rights pertaining to negotiable paper, he must have no notice of any such defects, must be actually innocent and ignorant of anything tending to show that the paper is invalid. Forn·al notice is not necessary. If he purchases a paper, knowing of such defects, he gets no better title than the one from whom he received it had.

IN THE USUAL COURSE OF BUSINESS.—Checks, drafts, and other negotiable instruments are passed from hand to hand as a daily occurrence in the payment of debts, making up of balances, and various other business transactions, and if a person procures the paper in the usual course of business he is presumed, so far as that is concerned, to have a good and sufficient title; but if he accepts a paper from an entire stranger, who asks for the loan of money and agrees to give the paper as security, it is not a business-like transaction, and not in the usual course of business, and such a transaction is sufficient to arouse the suspicions of an ordinarily prudent business man. In such a case, therefore, he can not be held to have received the paper in the ordinary course of business, and even though he may have paid value for it without actual notice of defects, still, if it should develop that there were defenses against its payment, or the paper was void, he would be obliged to suffer any loss rather than the maker.

BEFORE MATURITY.—Negotiable paper is presumed to be paid when due. If it is not paid when due, the law declares that it has lost its negotiability, and is thereafter mere assignable paper in the same manner as an ordinary written contract.'

Therefore, before a person can claim to be a bona-fide holder, and entitled to all his rights thereunder, he must show that he has obtained the paper before maturity. While the paper may pass from hand to hand by endorsement after maturity, its negotiability dies with the day of maturity, and no matter how much value the holder may pay, or how innocent he may be of any defects, or how regularly he may have received it, if he purchases after maturity, and the paper is void, he has no recourse against the maker.

If his endorser's title is good, his own will be good after maturity. If it is not good, his will not be good.

MATURITY.—What maturity is, is, in the light of what has been said, very important to know. When the time is stated in days, days, of course, must be counted, when it is in months, calendar months are meant.

In counting the time the date of the paper is excluded, and all of the last day is included.

A negotiable paper bearing interest, payable on demand, is due one year after its date, whether demanded or not; a note on demand without interest, matures six months after date.

TEST QUESTIONS.

1.   January 2nd, 1898.

On demand I promise to pay to J. Ross, or order, One Hundred ($100.00) Dollars with interest at one (1) per cent per month.   R. BOYD.

July 2d, 1898, the paper having circulated from hand to hand, comes into the possession of A. Is A a bona-fide holder so far as having received the paper before maturity is concerned?

2.   Stockton, August 1st, 1897.

On demand I promise to pay to J. Ross, or order, One Hundred ($100.00) Dollars.   R. BOYD.

December 1st, 1897, the note comes into the possession of A. So far as time is concerned is A a bona-fide holder?

CHAPTER XVII.

ENDORSEMENT.

DEFINITION.—We have seen that in accepting or certifying an instrument, the person so doing must write across the *face* of the instrument, while in endorsement he must write across the *back* of the instrument.

The place on the instrument where a name is written, to a large extent determines the purpose for which it is written.

Endorsement is the writing of one's name on the back of a negotiable instrument, with or without other words, with the purpose of transferring the title thereto.

The name when thus written also evidences the contract to transfer. In case of a paper made payable "to bearer," however, it is not necessary that the instrument should be endorsed in order to pass title, as the words "to bearer" in themselves give the title to whomever may be in possession of it, while all instruments payable "to order" must be endorsed.

WHO MAY ENDORSE.—Any competent party may endorse, the rule as to competent parties being the same as in ordinary contracts. Under these rules, a minor or person of unsound mind may avoid his endorsement if made, and may recover back his paper from his immediate endorsee, but after it gets into the hand of a third person, who is a bona-fide holder, the bona-fide holder is protected, and the minor or person of unsound mind has no right to recover his paper; and, as has been intimated before, even a thief or finder may endorse and pass a good title to a bona-fide holder, although he himself has no title.

If a person who has a right to endorse a paper dies, his legal representative may endorse the paper.

A paper owned by a partnership may be endorsed by any member of the firm signing the firm name.

FORM OF ENDORSEMENT.—

(1) In blank; as "R. Thomas."

(2) In full; as "Pay to R. Boyd, or order.

R. THOMAS."

(3) Without recourse: "Pay to R. Boyd, or order, without recourse to me. R. THOMAS."

or simply, "Without recourse.

R. THOMAS."

(4) Restrictive; "Pay to R. Boyd for collection.

R. THOMAS."

IN BLANK.—An endorsement in blank is one in which no endorsee is named, being simply the endorser's name written on the back of the paper.

This in legal effect is equivalent to making the paper payable "to bearer," but any lawful holder may afterwards turn a blank endorsement into a special one by writing above it a direction for payment to a particular person.

ENDORSEMENT IN FULL, as shown above, specifies the name of the person to whom it is to be paid, and prevents any one from transferring it except the person designated.

This form of endorsement is to be preferred to a blank endorsement as it affords security against fraud on the part of an unlawful holder, should the paper be lost, by making it necessary for the paper to have the signature of the person designated as endorsee.

WITHOUT RECOURSE.—When a person wishes to relieve himself from liability for payment as endorser, he uses the restrictive form of endorsement. The only effect this form of endorsement has is to relieve the endorser from liability for payment. It does not effect the negotiability of the instrument or relieve the endorser in any other way.

As shown above, either an endorsement in blank or an endorsement in full may be made without recourse.

RESTRICTIVE ENDORSEMENT.—It frequently happens that a person decides to transfer a note to another person merely for collection, or to be held as security, or for some temporary purpose, and wishes to prevent such person from transferring it to others. Such an endorsement in effect creates an agency and does not transfer the full title.

The endorser may however in turn endorse to a third person, but only by like restrictive endorsement, he having only a limited title; as agent himself, he can not convey more than the same limited title as agent.

ENDORSER'S LIABILITY.—Every endorser of a negotiable instrument, unless his endorsement is restricted, warrants to every subsequent holder thereof, who is not liable thereon to him,

(1) That it is in all respects what it purports to be;

(2) That he has a good title to it;

(3) That the signatures of all prior parties are binding upon them;

(4) That if the instrument is dishonored he will, upon proper notice, or without notice, where excused by law, pay the same.

Of course, as we have seen, a person who restricts his endorsement is not liable for the payment of the paper, but is liable on the first three warranties above stated.

The first three warranties are in the nature of original warranties, and if there is a breach of any of them, the party injured may proceed against the endorser at once.

The fourth warranty is conditional that if the paper is dishonored, the endorser will pay. This makes it necessary to present the paper to the maker and upon his refusal to pay, to give notice to the endorser.

These warranties must be taken, however, in connection with other rules concerning negotiable paper.

In the case of a check we have seen that the bank upon which it is drawn is absolutely responsible for the genuineness of the drawer's signature; so in this case the endorser is liable for the genuineness of the signature, if the bank pays on a forged signature.

ALLONGE.—After passing through many hands, a negotiable instrument sometimes has all available space filled with endorsements. In such a case it is permissible and lawful to paste a piece of blank paper on the end of the instrument, upon which other endorsements may be written. This is called an "Allonge."

TIME OF ENDORSEMENT.—As has been before explained, an endorsee, after maturity, takes the paper subject to all equities and defenses between the original parties, not however between other parties.

The fact that an instrument has arrived at maturity and has not been paid is a suspicious circumstance, sufficient to put any one on guard; and it is the law of negotiable instruments that they become at maturity, while not void, simply ordinary written contracts.

It must not be understood that the non-payment at maturity relieves the maker from the payment absolutely, but it allows him to present any legal defense, if any he have, against its payment.

AGAINST PRIOR ENDORSERS.—The holder even after maturity has a right of action for breach of the following general warranty in addition to the warranties above stated:

"One who sells an instrument thereby warrants that he has no knowledge of any facts which tend to prove it worthless, or its invalidity for any cause."

TEST QUESTIONS.

1.   Stockton, July 1st, 1898.

On demand we promise to pay One Hundred ($100.00) Dollars to J. Ross, or order.   R. BOYD,
                                                        D. STONE.

In the above note Stone claims to be liable only as an endorser. Are there any circumstances under which he might substantiate the claim? Discuss fully.

2. A holds a note to which he has forged B's name. A then sells the note to C, and endorses it "without recourse." B now proves the note to be forged. Can C collect it from A?

3. A, B and C are successive endorsers; each has endorsed "without recourse." D, a bona-fide holder, finds on presentment for payment that the note is a forgery. What are his rights if any against the prior endorsers and the maker?

4. A signs a note in favor of B, B knowing A at the time to be insolvent. B sells the note to C, after maturity, C being ignorant of the maker's insolvency. Has C any remedy against B?

CHAPTER XVIII.

PRESENTMENT AND NOTICE.

NECESSITY FOR.—It is not necessary to make presentment for payment to the principal debtor on a negotiable instrument in order to charge *him;* but it is necessary in order to hold the endorsers on an instrument to make demand of payment upon the principal debtor on the day of maturity, and upon his refusal to pay to notify the endorsers of such refusal.

PRESENTMENT—HOW MADE.—Presentment for payment must be made as follows, as nearly as by reasonable diligence it is practicable:

(1) By the holder;

(2) To the principal debtor at the place specified for payment, and if the debtor is not there, to any person having charge of such place;

(3) If no place is specified, wherever the debtor may be found;

(4) Upon the day of its maturity, or if on demand on any day, and within reasonable business hours.

If the debtor has no place of business, or if he can not with reasonable diligence be found, presentment is excused.

If the day of maturity falls on a holiday, presentment may be made on the next business day thereafter.

While it is not absolutely necessary, it is proper and a good business practice for the person who makes the presentment actually to show the paper to the debtor, and inform him that he is the holder and has come to demand payment, or words to that effect.

PROTEST.—When a maker or acceptor of an instrument refuses payment, the paper is said to be dishonored, and notice of the dishonor is given by protest.

(98)

This protest is a document containing a copy of the instrument, stating the presentment, the manner in which it was made, the presence or absence of the debtor, and his refusal to accept or pay, and the reason if any; and finally protesting against all the parties to be charged.

This protest must be made on the day of presentment, or on the next business day, and is made by a notary public, who makes a second presentment himself in order that he may personally certify to the dishonor of the instrument.

The notary then sends written notices of the fact of protest to the parties to the paper, and makes a statement on the protest of the names of the parties to whom he has sent notices.

All this given under the seal of the notary, is kept by the holder as evidence of presentment and dishonor.

It is not necessary to make a formal protest in the case of an inland bill, where the parties are near at hand, and proof is readily furnished; but the law requires that a foreign bill shall be formally protested, either before a notary public, as above described, or, if one can not be obtained, by any reputable person in the presence of two witnesses.

The notice of dishonor is not required to be in any particular form, and may be given,

(1) By delivering it to the party to be charged, or his agent, personally;

(2) By mailing the notice, postage prepaid, in time for the first mail which closes in the afternoon of the first business day succeeding the dishonor.

It is usual for a holder to give notice to all prior holders, but if he chooses to do so he may notify only the holder immediately preceding him. When this is done, that holder may in turn have a like time to notify his preceding holder and so on, one giving notice to the other until all are notified.

Of course, if the principal debtor pays the paper on presentment, all parties thereto are released from all obligations, and no protest or notice is had.

NOTICE—WHEN EXCUSED.—

(1) When the party by whom notice should be given, can not, with reasonable diligence, ascertain either the place of business, or residence of the party to be charged; or

(2) When there is no post-office communication between the towns where each resides, if in different towns;

(3) When the party to be charged is the person who dishonors the instrument; or

(4) When notice is waived by the party entitled thereto; notice of dishonor is excused.

It often happens that a paper is signed and several other parties immediately endorse it for the primary object of securing its payment. In such case it is customary for such endorsers to sign a statement like the following:

"We hereby waive demand of payment, protest, and notice;" and such a waiver is binding upon them, and relieves the holder from the trouble of making any demand, protest, or notice.

TEST QUESTIONS.

1. The maker of a negotiable instrument lives on a farm. The holder of such instrument on the day of maturity goes to the farm for the purpose of making presentment for payment. He finds that the maker is absent and can not learn his exact whereabouts. Under such circumstances can he give notice of presentment?

2. A draft falls due on Sunday. The next day is the Fourth day of July. Can presentment be lawfully made thereafter?

3. A holder attempts to give notice of protest by depositing a letter, properly addressed and prepaid, in the post-office before the post-office closes in the afternoon of the next day after the dishonor. The train which would regularly carry the letter, does not leave the station until the second day after the dishonor. Is the notice properly given?

CHAPTER XIX.

GUARANTY AND SURETYSHIP.

EXPLANATION.—Early in the history of the law there were material differences between a surety and a guarantor, but these differences have been so modified by statute that at present, so far as the legal status and legal liability are concerned, their positions are practically identical.

There are some differences yet remaining, but they are in the main merely formal, and not essential differences, so that we will consider the two as constituting but one subject.

A GUARANTY is a promise to answer for the debt, default, or miscarriage of another. It will be seen from the definition that the contract of guaranty is a contract annexed to, or placed upon another contract; e. g., A has made a contract by which he promises to pay a certain sum of money to B; C writes a statement upon this contract (or he may make it on a separate paper), to the effect that if A fails to pay the money, he himself will pay it.

LIABILITY.—It was further held that it was necessary that the guarantor should have notice of default on the part of his principal, but such is not now the law.

No notice is required and a guarantor is therefore absolutely liable immediately upon the default of the principal.

IN WRITING.—A contract of guaranty or suretyship must be in writing, except in case where the promise may be taken as being an original obligation, and where in fact the principal credit is given the guarantor himself; as in case A goes into a grocery store and says to the proprietor, "Send B certain groceries; I will pay for them;" while the grocer knows, of course, that the groceries are for B, and that A is to receive no benefit from them, still he may hold A as the principal debtor, under his own statement, without any contract in writing.

CONSIDERATION.—When a guaranty is entered into at the same time with the original obligation or with the acceptance of the latter by the guarantee, and forms with that obligation a part of the consideration to him, no other consideration need exist.

In all other cases there must be a consideration different from that of the original obligation, but the writing need not express the words "value received," or in any other way show a consideration. Consideration may be proved orally at any time when necessary. Of course, in all cases, being a contract, a guaranty requires a consideration.

KINDS.—Generally speaking there are three kinds of guaranties: of payment, of collection, and continuing guaranty.

GUARANTY OF PAYMENT.—One who guarantees the payment of a written instrument may write, "I guarantee the payment of the within instrument," or some such like words, and sign his name, or he may sign his name on the face of the instrument, beneath that of the maker, and add the words "surety" or "guarantor." He may even write his name on the back of an instrument in a similar manner as an endorser; but it is to be carefully noticed that he is not an endorser, and has not the right of notice which an endorser has in case of failure of the principal to pay.

His guaranty means that he will pay absolutely upon the failure of the principal debtor.

GUARANTY OF COLLECTION.—A guaranty to the effect that an obligation is good or collectible, imports that the debtor is solvent, and that the demand is collectible by the usual legal proceedings if taken with reasonable diligence.

In making such a guaranty the guarantor usually writes, "I hereby guarantee the collection of this note," and signs his name.

He becomes liable to pay the obligation only after a judgment has been obtained against the principal debtor, and an execution returned unsatisfied.

Thus we notice a distinction between the guaranty of payment and the guaranty of collection. In the case of guaranty of payment, mere refusal to pay makes the guarantor liable; while in guaranty of collection, the creditor must bring a suit and pursue it until the last legal procedure is had.

As to what is a reasonable time within which to commence suit, it has been held that the failure of the creditor to begin an action for six months after maturity of the obligation constitutes such negligence as will release the guarantor.

If it is shown, however, that at maturity and thereafter the principal debtor was insolvent, or has left the state or county, leaving no property therein not exempt from execution, the guarantor is liable without suit.

CONTINUING GUARANTY.—A guaranty relating to a future liability of the principal under successive transactions, is called a continuing guaranty, e. g., "I hereby guarantee the payment of all goods which The Stockton Paper Mills may hereafter sell to J. B. Ross, within six months from date hereof, and to the amount of Two Thousand ($2,000.00) Dollars; this to be taken as a continuing guaranty.
Dated July 21st, 1898.   (Signed) R. RYAN."

The above is the usual form of continuing guaranty. It may, however, be simply for a specified time, without stating an amount, or for an indefinite time, stating a specified amount.

This guaranty means that Ryan would be responsible for any Two Thousand Dollars worth of goods purchased during the six months.

The purchaser can therefore, after purchasing the full amount, pay off a part or all, and the guaranty is still valid for any further purchases up to the amount, and within the time.

A continuing guaranty may be revoked at any time by the guarantor in respect to future transactions.

EXONERATION OF GUARANTORS.—A guarantor is exonerated except so far as he may be indemnified by the principal, if by any act of the creditor without the consent of the guarantor the original obligation of the principal is altered in any respect, or the rights or remedies of the creditor against the principal in respect thereto, are in any way impaired or suspended; and the partial satisfaction of an obligation reduces the obligation of a guarantor to the same extent.

E. g., if in the case of continuing guaranty above given, the paper company should agree with J. B. Ross to extend credit to him for purchases beyond the six months' life of the guaranty, that would be such a relinquishment of the right to sue Ross during the six months as would also relieve the guarantor from liability for payment, unless he agreed that the credit should be given.

A guarantor's obligation is extinguished also if he performs or offers to perform the obligation resting upon him in accordance with the contract, and such performance is refused.

Such a case comes under the general rule of good tender, which we have before considered. In any event a guarantor can not be held beyond the express terms of his contract.

The ordinary ways in which a guarantor may be discharged from his liability are,

(1) Expiration of time, on a continuing guaranty;

(2) Notice from the guarantor;

(3) Alteration of the agreement, such as substituting different goods for the ones for which payment is guaranteed;

(4) Giving time to the principal; and

(5) Fraud practised upon the guarantor by the creditor or by the debtor with the creditor's consent.

Fraud practised upon the guarantor by the debtor, without the knowledge of the creditor, will not release the guarantor, but gives him a right of action against the debtor for damages for the fraud.

REMEDIES OF PARTIES.—As we have seen, if the prin-

cipal debtor fails to perform his obligation the creditor may sue
the guarantor at once, and if the guarantor is compelled to pay
the creditor, he in turn has a right to sue the principal debtor;
having paid his debt for him, he has a right to demand reimbursement.

CONTRIBUTION.—Where, as often happens, there are several guarantors or sureties, each one is liable for all of the debt
and the creditor may compel any one to pay all of the debt.   Any
guarantor who is thus compelled to pay all of the debt, may in
turn compel each of his co-sureties to contribute their proportion
of the debt to reimburse him.   This is known as contribution
among sureties or guarantors.

TEST QUESTIONS.

1. A enters a store with B.   B orders some goods for himself.   A says to the merchant, "If B does not pay for those
   goods I will."   B fails to pay for them.   What right of
   collection, if any, has the merchant against A?

2. A guarantees the payment by B of $1,000 for goods pur-
   chased within one year's time.   On the last day of the
   year B purchased goods at thirty days' time.   Can the
   wholesaler hold A for the goods?   Discuss the question
   fully.

3. A wholesaler and his customer A go to B together and A
   makes this statement, "The wholesaler will furnish me a
   choice, well-selected stock of fresh groceries to the amount
   of $5,000 if you will guarantee the payment."   B agrees
   and gives a written guaranty.   The wholesaler ships groceries to A, knowing that they are not salable nor fresh.
   A fails to pay for the groceries.   Is B liable on his guaranty?   Discuss fully.

CHAPTER XX.

INTEREST AND USURY.

INTEREST is the compensation allowed by law or fixed by the parties for the use, or forbearance, or detention of money.

This subject is especially important to every one, and the definition just stated should be carefully examined.

It will be noticed that it is compensation either allowed by law, or fixed by the parties; hence under the definition any rate fixed by the parties is allowable by law.

A common transaction is borrowing money and paying interest thereon for the *use* of money, but the law allows interest in cases where people refuse or neglect to pay money which they are lawfully entitled to pay, as in case where a judgment is obtained against a person and he declines to pay the amount of the judgment.

He may not be using the money; he may not even have the money with which to pay, nevertheless interest is charged against him because he *detains* money from the person who holds the judgment against him.

Interest is usually a certain per cent upon the principal sum, and unless otherwise stated, is presumed by law to be annual. It is usual to state definitely in the contract that the interest is to be at a certain rate per cent per annum, or per month.

"Ten per cent per annum," means an interest of $10 on each $100 for each year the money is used or detained.

LEGAL RATE.—The legal rate, unless there is an express contract in writing fixing a definite rate, is seven per cent per annum. This applies to all money due.

The laws of the different states provide for different rates, some states limiting the amount to a certain rate.

The law of the place where the contract for payment of interest is made, however, will govern in the payment thereof, unless it is expressly provided in the instrument that the principal and interest are payable in some different place.

ON WHAT ALLOWED.—Interest is allowed by agreement on all forms of debt, from the time of the creation of the debt until it is paid; or it may begin at any time after the creation of the debt, or after the debt is due, and in any event where no express agreement is made interest is allowed on all claims as soon as they are due and remain unpaid, and on all judgments.

For example; if goods are sold "for cash" and cash is not paid, interest may be collected from the date of the sale until payment. If they are sold on sixty days' time, interest begins at the expiration of the sixty days.

COMPOUND INTEREST.—Compound interest is allowed only where there is a special agreement therefor by the parties, evidenced by a contract in writing. They may agree that the interest may be paid yearly, semi-annually, or even monthly, and if not so paid when due it may be added to the principal and become a part thereof, and bear interest at the same rate.

USURY is the taking of higher interest, or the agreement to take or give higher interest than the law provides.

This, as we have noticed by a careful study of the definition of interest, can not apply in California, as any rate of interest may be allowed by agreement.

In some states, however, the law forbids the taking of any greater than the legal rate, and provides penalties therefor.

TEST QUESTIONS.

1. A signs a note as follows:

June 1st, 1896.

One day after date I promise to pay to J. Brown, or order, One Hundred ($100) Dollars, without interest.

R. CAINE.

May interest be at any time collected on the note?

CHAPTER XXI.

SALES OF PERSONAL PROPERTY.

INTRODUCTION.—Property is anything which has value, and is susceptible of ownership; air, for example, has value, but is not susceptible to ownership, while land complies with the requirements of the definition.

Property is divided with respect to kind into two general classes, real and personal property.

Real property will be discussed fully in a subsequent chapter.

Personal property, while difficult of exact definition, may be said to be generally movable property, such as live stock, furniture, vehicles, and musical instruments. Even where property is considered immovable, such as a house, yet if it is actually moved, it is considered as personal property; or a house may be considered as personal property, even while remaining affixed to the soil, if it is placed upon the land for a mere temporary purpose, and to be removed.

Trees are considered real property while growing. As soon as cut down, are considered personal property.

Annual crops, however, such as wheat and barley, are considered personal property, and may be sold or mortgaged as such even while growing.

TRADE-MARK.—One who make a business of selling a particular article may, by his skill in preparing or handling such article, procure for it a large sale and great profit to himself. When such is the case, and he desires to prevent others from imitating his goods, or selling similar goods under like name, he may use what is called a trade-mark.

(109)

A trade-mark is any word, letter, device, emblem, or symbol affixed by any tradesman to denote any goods sold by him, other than any words denoting a class or description.

In order to be effective a person so claiming a trade-mark must file with the Secretary of State, or with the Commissioner of Patents in the United States Patent Office, a copy or description of such trade-mark, accompanied by his fee for filing of $3.00 to the State, or $25 to the United States.

A trade-mark thus filed is personal property, and subject to sale as other personal property.

INFRINGEMENT OF TRADE-MARK.—Any one who uses a forged trade-mark with a wilful intent to deceive or defraud is guilty of a misdemeanor, and may be punished accordingly; and the phrase "forged trade-mark" includes every alteration or imitation of any trade-mark, so nearly resembling the original as to be likely to deceive.

Any one infringing a trade-mark, in addition to the penal offense committed, is also liable in damage to whatever extent the rightful owner of the trade-mark may suffer by reason of the infringement.

DEFINITION.—A sale is a contract by which for a pecuniary consideration called a price, one transfers to another an interest in property. By analyzing this definition we see that a sale is a contract, and hence liable to all rules regarding contracts; and further that the consideration is pecuniary.

"Price" means "money." A contract in which the consideration is goods or merchandise is called "barter," and thirdly we notice that the sale is a transfer of an interest in property, so that a sale can be completed even before the property itself changes hands.

SUBJECT MATTER.—One of the essential elements of every contract, as we have learned, is subject matter.

In the sale of personal property this subject matter must be either in actual existence, or in potential, or probable, existence;

as for example, A during the winter makes a sale of peaches which he expects to have on his trees the following summer. The peaches in this case are in potential or probable existence. If, however, the crop should.fail for any cause, the sale will become void, because of failure of subject matter, and the purchaser may recover any moneys paid, and rescind his contract.

A similar case is where the parties have entered into a contract of sale in regard to something which has ceased to exist, in ignorance of that fact; as where A has bought a horse from B, and at the time of making the sale the horse was dead. A can recover the price paid and avoid the sale on the ground of no subject matter.

The same is true where the subject matter is partly destroyed, as in case of goods damaged by fire or otherwise.

ILLEGAL SUBJECT MATTER.—This subject has already been discussed in a previous chapter, and the same rule applies to the subject matter of sales as to any other contract.

The subject matter, however, is considered to be legal unless the law especially declares it to be illegal.

The sale of obscene and immoral publications is an instance of illegal subject matter prohibited by law, and the sale of such matter so prohibited is absolutely void, and neither party has any recourse against the other; the seller for the recovery of the price, or the buyer for non-delivery of the writing.

PARTIES.—The parties to a sale must be competent parties, under the general rule of parties to contracts. In the contract of sale the particular names given are seller or vendor, and buyer or vendee.

STATUTE OF FRAUDS.—The particular portion of the Statute of Frauds which refers to the sale of personal property, or an agreement to buy or sell, is as follows:—

No sale of personal property, or agreement to buy or sell it for a price of $200 or more, is valid, unless,

(1) The agreement, or some note or memorandum thereof, be in writing, and subscribed by the party to be charged, or by his agent; or

(2) The buyer accepts and receives part of the thing sold;

(3) The buyer at the time of the sale pays a part of the price.

By a careful analysis of the above it will be seen that the statute contains very just provisions in regard to sales, and at the same time makes sales of small amounts easy to consummate.

SUBDIVISION ONE.—It is not necessary that there should be a special formal agreement in writing. A mere note or memorandum is sufficient, and it need not be subscribed by both parties. The person who gives the note or memorandum only need subscribe, or write his name *under*, the memorandum.

A formal Bill of Sale, as it is called, is often made, however, in which is stated formally that the vender sells to the vendee at a certain price certain described property, and in which he warrants that he has title to the same.

The vender signing the instrument can be held liable under its terms, while it can not be enforced against the vendee unless he has also signed it.

SUBDIVISION TWO.—If the buyer accepts and receives part of the thing sold, this does away with the necessity of any writing.

The fact that he has taken part of the goods as his own, the law declares to be sufficient evidence that he has bought them, and no writing or further proof is required.

SUBDIVISION THREE.—This is similar to subdivision two. If the vendee pays at the time part of the price, or all of it, this is held to be sufficient to make a valid sale without regard to any writing or actual delivery of the goods.

Examples: A wishes to buy fifty tons of hay at $10 per ton. We see at a glance that the amount is over $200, hence there are three ways in which he can make a valid purchase.

First: He may secure a written instrument from B, the vender, without paying anything, or even seeing the hay.

Second: He may go and take a wagon load of the hay and transfer it to his own premises without any writing; or

Third: He may pay a part of the $500 without any writing, or without receiving any of the hay. In either of the three cases a valid sale is consummated.

AUCTION SALES.—A sale by auction is a sale by public outcry to the highest bidder on the spot.

It is complete when the auctioneer publicly announces by the fall of his hammer or in any other customary manner that the thing is sold. Until he makes such announcement any bidder may withdraw his bid.

IN WRITING.—An auction sale of course must conform to the Statute of Frauds in regard to sales, and when property is sold by auction an entry made by the auctioneer or his clerk in his sale book at the time of the sale, specifying the names of the vendor and the vendee, the thing sold, the price and terms of sale, binds both parties in the same manner as if made by themselves. In such sales the auctioner is considered as the agent of both parties.

BY BIDDING.—This is the employment, by a seller, of any person to bid without an intention on the part of such bidder to buy, and on the part of the seller to enforce his bid, and is such a fraud upon the buyer as entitles him to rescind his purchase; or when he discovers the fraud he may demand the property on tender of the amount of the highest bona-fide bid. For example, A is a bona-fide bidder. He bids $50 on a horse; B, a bona-fide bidder, bids $60 on the horse; A then bids $70; C, a by-bidder, continues to bid against A until $100 is reached, and the horse declared sold to A for that price. If A discovers the fraud he can compel the sale of the horse to him upon tendering $70, the amount of his highest bid against B, the only other bona-fide bidder.

8

An owner of property or his agent has a right as a matter of course to bid on his own goods if he does so fairly and openly, unless he has announced, or the auctioneer has announced by his authority, that the sale is to be without limit or reserve, or makes any equivalent declaration.

TEST QUESTIONS.

1. A water-trough is imbedded in the ground. Discuss the question as to whether it is personal or real property.
2. A makes a contract with B for the purchase of twenty tons of hay at $5.00 per ton, to be hauled by A from a large stack until the full twenty tons is supplied. A afterwards refuses to take the hay. Is he liable in damages?

CHAPTER XXII.

DELIVERY.

TRANSFER OF TITLE.—Ownership or title is an intangible thing. The only way we can tell that a person owns a thing, or has title to it, is by the conduct of himself and others in regard to that thing.

As we have seen in the preceding chapter, the sale of personal property of the value of $200, or over, must be evidenced by certain acts, and when these acts are done, the title, poetically speaking, wings its flight in spirit from the vendor to the vendee.

VALUE LESS THAN $200.—In case where the property is less than $200 in value, the usual evidence of the title having passed, is the delivery of the property the subject of the sale. Unless credit is extended by agreement, all sales are presumed to be for cash.

DELIVERY means,

(1) The actual changing of the possession from the vendor to the vendee of the article sold; or

(2) In cases where the article sold is of such great bulk as to be difficult of actual delivery, a symbol may be passed. As, if bales of cotton are sold, the key of the warehouse in which it is stored, may be delivered instead of the cotton.

This amounts to a delivery of the cotton itself, and is called Constructive Delivery.

DELIVERY, HOW MADE.—A vendor must put personal property into a condition fit for delivery, and deliver it to the buyer within a reasonable time after demand.

Delivery, however, does not mean that the vender shall carry

(115)

the property to the vendee's residence, or place of business, but in absence of any agreement, personal property sold is deliverable at the place where it is at the time of the sale, or agreement to sell, or if it is not then in existence it is deliverable at the place where it is produced.

If the vendor agrees to send the thing sold to the vendee's place of business or residence, he must follow the directions of the latter as to the manner of sending. If he does not, he is liable for its damage.

If he follows such directions and uses ordinary care in forwarding the article, it is at the risk of the buyer.

EXAMPLES.—A buys kerosene at a grocery store with the intention of carrying it away himself. As soon as the kerosene is drawn and set out on the counter within reach of A, it amounts to a delivery to him.

If he orders the kerosene sent to his house in the grocer's delivery wagon, and through the driver's carelessness the kerosene is lost en route, it is not a delivery, and the grocer must stand the loss.

Suppose further that the oil is to be sent by the grocer's wagon, and while on the way lightning strikes the can and the oil is lost.

This being without fault of the grocer, the oil is considered as having been delivered, and A must stand the loss.

DELIVERY BY SEGREGATION.—This is a case of actual delivery where it is sometimes difficult to tell whether a delivery has been made, and a great deal of litigation has been had to determine what constitutes a segregation or delivery of goods that are not easily carried away at the time of the sale; e. g., if A goes to B and agrees on a price he will pay for fifty bags of wheat, which are with other bags of wheat in a large pile, the question always arises in the event of the failure to take the wheat, or in the event of its destruction, whether at the time of the contract, the wheat was delivered,

The rule in this regard is as follows: If at the time of the contract, fifty bags of wheat were separated from the pile, or so marked and designated so that A knew exactly which fifty sacks of wheat were his, such segregation or marking would constitute a legal delivery.

On the other hand if no such marking or segregation was had, there was no delivery, and in case all of the wheat was destroyed before A removed the fifty bags, B must lose all, as he can not specify any particular wheat as belonging to A.

The general rule in the abstract is as follows: "When anything remains to be done by the vendor to the goods before they are ready for the vendee, the title does not pass, and it is not a delivery until such thing is done."

DELIVERY TO CARRIER.—Merchants in the west frequently purchase large quantities of goods in eastern cities, which are sent across the continent by rail.

The railroad companies are known as common carriers, and a delivery of goods by a New York merchant, properly packed, marked, and in good condition, is considered a delivery to the merchant in the west, particularly if the buyer's directions as to what route the goods are to be sent, are followed.

In case then of a wreck or fire by which the goods are destroyed en route, the seller would be relieved of any liability, and would not suffer the loss.

STOPPAGE IN TRANSITU.—Taking the cases just above cited of the purchase from the New York merchant of goods, it is a rule of law that notwithstanding that delivery to the common carrier is a delivery of the goods to the western merchant, and that the western merchant must bear the loss if any be suffered; yet if the price of the goods has not been paid, and the vender learns of the vendee's insolvency before the goods reach the vendee, he may notify the carrier to stop the goods and return them to him.

This right, however, can only be exercised under the following circumstances.

(1) Debt must be for the identical goods shipped.

(2) Goods must be in carrier's hands.

(3) Vendee must be insolvent.

IN TRANSIT.—Literally we understand that when goods are in transit, they are actually moving, or in the process of carriage from one place to another, but so far as concerns the right of stoppage in transitu, the goods are in transit even after they have reached their destination and are in the warehouse or freight station of the carrier.

At any time therefore before the delivery into the actual or constructive possession of the buyer, the right may be exercised.

If, however, the buyer has the actual possession, or the key of the warehouse (constructive possession), the right is at an end.

THE DEBT.—It must be carefully remembered that the goods can not be stopped on account of a general balance due, but the money must be owing on the identical goods.

Even if a part payment has been made on the goods, they may be stopped. And where a note has been given for the purchase price, the goods may be stopped, as a note is not a payment, but mere evidence of the debt.

If part of the price of the goods has been paid, and the vendor stops the goods in transit, he must either return the portion paid or relinquish such part of the goods as the debtor may demand as the equivalent of the price, if the goods are of such material as to be severable. Of course, if he is tendered the full amount of the price by the debtor, he must release the goods.

THE INSOLVENCY.—By insolvency is meant when a person ceases to pay his debts in the manner usual with persons of his business, or when he declares his inability or unwillingness to do so.

It is not necessary that the vendor should wait until the vendee be declared an insolvent by a Court. Such a delay would defeat the right of stoppage entirely. The insolvency, or at any rate the vendor's knowledge of the insolvency, must have been after the shipment of the goods. If he sells goods, knowing the purchaser to be insolvent, he does so at his peril.

STOPPAGE, HOW EFFECTED.—The vendor may take actual possession of the goods himself, or he may give notice to the carrier or his agent who has immediate possession of the goods.

In the case above referred to, a telegram sent to the conductor of a train or an agent through whose hands the goods must pass before reaching their destination would be sufficient, and if the carrier delivers the goods to the vendee after receiving such notice he is liable in damages to the vendor.

The following is the ordinary form of such notice:—

New York City, Sept. 21, 1898.

To Wells, Fargo & Co.,

Agent at San Francisco,

Dear Sir: On the 19th inst. I delivered to you two cases of dry goods marked and consigned to J. Ross, San Francisco, California. Certain things have arisen which give me the right of stoppage in transitu. I therefore hereby instruct you not to deliver these goods, but to hold them subject to my further order.

J. Dalton.

LEGAL EFFECT.—Stoppage in transitu does not of itself rescind the sale, but is a means of enforcing the lien of the seller for the price of the goods. Until further action is taken, therefore, the vendor does not recover title to the goods by recovering possession, but simply holds them to satisfy his lien for the' purchase price.

BILL OF LADING.—A bill of lading is a written memorandum, signed by the carrier, stating that certain goods have been received for shipment, with the names of the consignor and the consignee, and an agreement upon his part to deliver them to the consignee.

This bill of lading is usually made in duplicate, one copy being sent to the consignee; and upon presenting it to the carrier, the carrier is ordinarily bound to deliver to him the goods named therein.

In case of stoppage in transitu, however, the carrier is under no obligation to deliver the goods to an insolvent vendee, even if he does produce a bill of lading, but it often happens that a bill of lading is received by the vendee many days before the goods arrive, and if he sells the bill of lading to a bona-fide purchaser, the right of stoppage in transitu can not afterwards be exercised so as to defeat the rights of the innocent holder of the bill of lading.

While a bill of lading has not all the elements of a negotiable instrument, nevertheless the law provides that it may pass to a bona-fide holder in like manner as a bill of exchange.

FRAUDULENT SALES.—In order to defraud creditors, a person owing sums of money often seeks to dispose of his property by a formal sale with the understanding, express or implied, that the property or its equivalent, is to be returned to him. The law especially provides, however, that all such sales, or attempted sales, are void, and declares that unless such sale is accompanied by immediate delivery, and followed by actual and continued change of possession, it is void as against creditors.

In certain instances, however, where actual delivery is difficult, the law allows such a transfer to be evidenced by a written document, stating the fact of the sale, which must be recorded in the office of the County Recorder in the County where the property is situated.

Even when these directions of the law are followed, the sale can be set aside at the instance of the creditors if they can show that the sale has been consummated for the purpose of defrauding them.

TEST QUESTIONS.

1. A and B were conversing in regard to a horse. A said, "I will give you $50 for that horse in the corral." B replies, "Agreed. There is your horse." Was there a delivery of the horse sufficient to constitute a sale?

2. A ordered a harvesting machine from B. While in a half-finished state the machine was destroyed. Whose loss is it?

3. A gives a bill of sale of his grocery store to B. B came to the store, but A did not remove. A's signs were not removed. Was there a delivery of the store as against creditors of A?

4. A vendor of goods learns after they are shipped that the vendee is insolvent. State fully how he may protect himself from the effect of the vendee's insolvency.

5. Goods are shipped from Boston to San Francisco. Upon their arrival, the Railroad Company places them in their warehouse and notifies the consignee that the goods are at his disposal. Before the goods are removed the carrier receives notice from the vendor to hold them. Explain the rights of the parties.

6. A vendor, under proper circumstances, notifies a carrier to hold goods. Before the date of such notice, the vendee has received and sold the Bill of Lading for a small part of the value of the goods, and immediately thereafter declared himself insolvent. Discuss the rights of the parties.

CHAPTER XXIII.

WARRANTY.

DEFINITION.—A warranty is an engagement by which a seller assures to a buyer the existence of some fact affecting the transaction, whether past, present, or future.

This assurance or warranty is, of course, a contract. It is usually made at the time the contract of sale is entered into, and the consideration for the principal contract is the consideration for the warranty. If made independently of the contract of sale, it requires a separate consideration.

Warranties may be express or implied.

EXPRESS WARRANTY consists of a warranty expressly stated in words. All statements, however, made by the vendor for the purpose of inducing another to buy, are not warranties.

All such expressions as, "These are the finest peaches raised in the State," or "This is the handsomest horse I ever saw," are mere dealer's talk, expressions of his opinion, and not warranties.

The test of a warranty is, "Did the vendor assume to assert a fact of which the vendee was ignorant, or did he merely intend to give his opinion?"

By a careful study of the general definition of warranty and the test above given, it will be seen that a vendor can not be chargeable with a breach of warranty, even if he wilfully misstates some material fact, provided the vendee is not deceived.

IMPLIED WARRANTIES.—It would be inconvenient and extremely annoying to both parties if the buyer, in order to protect himself, was required to procure, or the seller to give, express warranties concerning the subject matter of every sale.

(122)

Hence the law in certain cases declares that by the very act of selling goods, a vendor gives certain warranties.

The following are implied warranties on the part of the vendor:

(1) That he has a good and unincumbered title to the property.

(2) If sold by sample, that the quality of the bulk shall be equal to the quality of the sample.

(3) That provisions sold by a regular dealer for domestic use to an actual consumer are sound and wholesome.

(4) If he has manufactured an article, he warrants that it is free from any defects not disclosed, arising from the process of manufacture, and that proper materials have been used therein.

(5) That an article manufactured for a particular purpose is reasonably fit for that purpose.

(6) That merchandise inaccessible to the buyer, is sound and merchantable.

(7) Generally, a seller impliedly warrants that neither he nor his agent knows of any fact concerning the thing sold which would destroy the buyer's inducement to buy.

REMARKS.—Under subdivision three above, it will be noted that there is no implied warranty in the case of a wholesale dealer in provisions selling to a retail dealer, while there is a warranty from the retailer to the person who buys for his own use. There are good reasons for this distinction.

The retailer is presumed to be an expert judge of wholesome provisions, and to inspect them before accepting them, and as he does not necessarily consume any of them himself, no personal injury may come to him through unwholesome provisions.

It must also be carefully noted that the provisions must be sold by a regular retail dealer, or there is no warranty, and it has been held that it is only when the provisions are sold for immediate consumption, that the warranty applies. If the purchaser holds them indefinitely before attempting to use them, he can not then claim the benefit of implied warranty if he finds them unwholesome.

Under subdivision five, it is to be noted that an article manufactured for a purpose is only required to be ordinarily or reasonably fit for the purpose.

It need not be the best article or machine for the purpose, but it is sufficient if it is reasonably fit. Thus, if a man contracts for the manufacture of a gun which will shoot half a mile, and the gun is produced that will shoot half a mile with a reasonable degree of precision, the warranty is satisfied, even though there may be many other guns which will shoot half a mile with a far greater degree of precision.

The general implied warranty, stated in subdivision seven, covers a multitude of cases of warranty; e. g., a horse dealer may know that a particular horse, which he is offering for sale, has inherited tender feet, and in all probability will go lame upon being driven.

Under the first six implied warranties, he is freed from any responsibility, but under the last, if a purchaser can show the dealer's knowledge of the defect in the horse, he may recover for breach of warranty.

EXPRESS STATEMENT CONTROLS IMPLIED.—While it is true that where no express warranty is given, the above considered implied warranties are always in effect, yet any of these implied warranties may be set aside and superseded by an express statement in regard to the transaction; for instance, if a provision dealer expressly says that he does not warrant certain provisions to be wholesome, the buyer then buys them without any implied warranty as to their fitness for use.

CAVEAT EMPTOR, meaning, "Let the purchaser beware," enters largely into the question of whether a vendor has been guilty of breach of warranty or not.

Every person is presumed to exercise the degree of skill in his business transactions which is customary with ordinarily prudent persons in like transactions, and if he does not do so, implied warranties will not protect him, as the law declares that a general warranty does not extend to defects inconsistent therewith of which the buyer was then aware, or which were then easily discernible by him without the exercise of peculiar skill.

This general rule, however correct it may be, is somewhat difficult of application. Ordinary skill or discernment might be charged against a person familiar with the subject matter, and not against a person unfamiliar; e. g., A having no special knowledge of horses, goes to a dealer and tells him he wants a sound horse. He picks out a horse apparently sound, but which the dealer well knew was diseased. In such case the dealer is guilty of breach of warranty, notwithstanding the purchaser's presence and examination of the horse.

Suppose, however, that a professional horseman went to the dealer, examined and selected a horse, which afterwards proved to be diseased. He would have no remedy against the dealer for breach of implied warranty, if by using the ordinary skill used by people in his line of business he could have discovered the condition of the horse.

In the case of provisions, if a customer views a certain box of potatoes and tells the dealer to send that particular box of potatoes to his residence, he can not afterwards claim breach of warranty if the potatoes are unfit for use. If, on the contrary, he merely orders a box of potatoes without seeing them, the dealer is bound under his general warranty to furnish sound and wholesome potatoes.

BREACH OF WARRANTY.—When a vendor violates any of the warranties above mentioned there is said to be a breach of warranty on his part, and he is so far responsible for such breach of warranty that the buyer has a remedy against him, and is entitled to recover to the extent of the injury suffered.

There are three remedies under the varying conditions of the sale:

(1) If the goods are neither received nor paid for, the buyer may refuse either to receive or pay for them.

(2) If goods are received and paid for, he may sue for damages for breach of the warranty; or

(3) If goods are received and not paid for, set up damage as a counter claim against the vendor's action for the price.

TEST QUESTIONS.

1. A grower sold seed in packages marked "Large Bristol Cabbage Seed;" it proved to be cabbage seed of an inferior and worthless variety. Has the vendee any right of action against the vendor?

2. Goods sold by sample were delivered to the vendee; the vendee on inspecting the goods found that they did not come up to the sample. Discuss his right to reject the goods.

3. A furniture dealer assures a customer that a certain table is of walnut. The customer is familiar with the wood and knows that it is oak. He, however, says nothing but purchases the table and afterward claims a breach of warranty on the part of the dealer in saying that the table was walnut. All the facts being shown, discuss his right to recover against the dealer.

4. A dealer sells a plow to A for plowing ordinarily tillable soil. It is so made that the share will not stay in the ground. Has the buyer any remedy?

5. A steals a wagon and sells it to B. The true owner compels B to restore it. What remedy has B?

6. A sells a wagon to B, and at the same time states that the title to the wagon is in dispute, and that he will not be responsible for a return of the price if it should be determined that he is not the owner. It is so determined. Has B any remedy?

CHAPTER XXIV.

CONDITIONAL SALES AND MORTGAGES.

DEFINITION.—A conditional sale is a sale in which the title is vested, defeated, or modified upon the occurrence of an uncertain event.

These events may be

(1) Precedent;

(2) Concurrent; or

(3) Subsequent

to the agreement for sale.

(1) If A agrees that he will hold certain goods subject to B's order, and upon the condition that B will pay a debt of old standing, the title passes as soon as B has paid the old debt. The payment of the old debt is the condition preceding the passing of the title.

(2) Conditions concurrent are those which are mutually dependent, and are to be performed at the same time; as in the case of cash sales the delivery of the goods and payment of the cash are concurrent conditions.

(3) Conditions subsequent refer to a future event upon the happening of which the obligation becomes no longer binding; as the sale of land to become void if the title of the vendor proves to be defective.

SALES ON TRIAL.—This is a form of sale on condition precedent, the condition being that the article sold prove satisfactory for the purpose for which it was bought.

Such sales are usually made on trial for a certain specified time, and if the time elapses and the purchaser does not return the goods, the sale becomes absolute; or in the absence of a special agreement, a reasonable time for trial is allowed. What is reasonable time depends on the circumstances in each case.

In such sale if the purchaser, in the course of trying, breaks, injures, or destroys the article, the question at once arises, Who must bear the loss?

The rule is as follows: "If the purchaser gave the article such trial only as articles reasonably fit for such purposes ordinarily stand without breaking, the loss falls on the vendor. On the contrary if the purchaser negligently and carelessly or improperly uses the article, and it is thereby broken, the loss falls on the purchaser."

SALES BY SAMPLE are conditional sales, there being a precedent condition that the quality of the bulk shall equal the quality of the sample.

This class of sales has been discussed under the head of Warranty, and it will be noted that such sales are both sales under warranty and conditional sales.

SALES OF GOODS TO ARRIVE.—In long ocean voyages it sometimes happens that vendees sell out their business or change their occupation. while the goods are on the way.

In such cases it is customary to make the sale of the goods conditional upon their arrival. The sale becomes absolute when the goods arrive. If they never arrive, the sale is void; and a reasonable time only is allowed for the goods to arrive.

A sale may, of course, be made of goods to arrive, without the condition, which will be absolute in the beginning. In such case the buyer must take his chances. If the goods do not arrive, the loss falls upon him.

If no agreement is made at all in regard to the matter, the loss will fall on the buyer.

A CHATTEL MORTGAGE is a contract by which specific personal property is hypothecated for the performance of an act, without the necessity of a change of possession.

It is the law in some states, and was so under the old common law system, that chattel mortgages were mere sales on condition, but our modern law has changed the form to agree with the fact, and made mortgages mere liens on property given as security, instead of indulging in the fiction of a sale, and depriving the true owner of the possession of his property.

It will be seen that a mortgage gives a special lien, and that, it is not necessary for the mortgagee to have possession of the property.

Of course, there is nothing to prevent a person making a conditional sale of any property he may have, with the understanding that the sale is to become void upon the payment of some amount, or other condition fulfilled.

IN WRITING.—A chattel mortgage can only be created, renewed, or extended by a writing executed with the formalities required in the case of a grant of real property; that is, it must be acknowledged before some officer qualified to administer oaths, and recorded in the office of the county Recorder of the county in which the property mortgaged is situated; and further accompanied by an affidavit of all the parties thereto that it was made in good faith and without any design to hinder, delay, or defraud creditors.

FORM.—A mortgage of personal property may be made in substantially the following form:—

"This mortgage, made the 1st day of September, in the year One Thousand Eight Hundred and Ninety-eight, by A B, of Stockton, California, by occupation a farmer, mortgagor, to C D, of the same place, by occupation a grain dealer, mortgagee;

"Witnesseth: That the mortgagor mortgages to the mortgagee all that certain personal property situated and described as follows, to wit:—

"Being one two-horse spring wagon, one spring-tooth harrow, one Gorham seed-sower, all situated on what is known as the A B ranch near Stockton, in San Joaquin County, California, as

9

security for the payment to said C D, the mortgagee, of One Hundred ($100.00) Dollars on the 1st day of February, in the year One Thousand Eight Hundred and Ninety-nine, with interest thereon at the rate of Ten (10) per cent per annum, according to the terms and conditions of a certain promissory note, of even date herewith, a copy of which is as follows:

"September 1, 1898.

"February 1, 1899, after date, I promise to pay to C D, or order, One Hundred ($100.00) Dollars with interest at the rate of ten (10) per cent per annum, from date hereof until paid.

"A B.

"IN WITNESS WHEREOF, The said mortgagor has hereunto set his hand the day and year first above written.

"A B."

The form of oath annexed to the mortgage proper, is as follows:—

State of California,   } ss.
County of San Joaquin. }

A B, the mortgagor in the foregoing mortgage named, and C D, the mortgagee in said mortgage named, each being duly sworn each for himself, doth depose and say: That the aforesaid mortgage is made in good faith and without any design to hinder, delay, or defraud any creditor or creditors.

A B,
C D.

Subscribed and sworn to before me this 1st day of September, 1898, in the County of San Joaquin.

[SEAL]   E F, Notary Public.

ACKNOWLEDGMENT is simply for the purpose of affording good evidence that the mortgagor signed the mortgage, and rendering it improbable that he will ever dispute his signature.

An acknowledgment is taken thus. In the above example A B appears before the notary personally with the mortgage fully

drawn up and signed (or he may sign it in the notary's presence)
and says to the notary, "I acknowledge this to be my signature.
I signed it to this mortgage for the purpose of mortgaging the
property therein described," or some such like words. No form
of words is required so long as A B sufficiently admits his signature and its purpose. The notary will then affix to the mortgage
his certificate to the effect .that A B acknowledged to him the
execution or signing of the mortgage. The mortgage may then
be recorded.

RECORDING.—So far as the parties to the instrument are
concerned, the mortgage would be valid between them without
being recorded, or even without the affidavit annexed, but in
order to protect the mortgagee against other creditors, he must
see that the mortgage is recorded in the office of the County
Recorder of the county in which the property mortgaged is situated, and also of the county in which the mortgagor resides.

If the property be partly in different counties, the mortgage
must be recorded in each county.

A mortgagor who removes the mortgaged property from the
county in which it was mortgaged, without the written consent of
the mortgagee, and with the intent to defraud the mortgagee, is
guilty of the crime of larceny, and may be punished accordingly.

As the only effect of recording is to give notice to the world
that the property has been mortgaged, and that therefore there is
a lien or claim upon the property by some one, other than the
legal owner, it follows that even if the mortgage is not recorded
any one who has actual notice of the mortgage can not claim any
right to the property as against the mortgagee, other than he
would have had if the mortgage had been recorded.

FORECLOSURE is regularly had by bringing a suit and getting a judgment authorizing the sale of the property by the Sheriff or Constable.

It is often provided in the mortgage, however, that in case of
default the mortgagee may take possession and sell. When he

does so take possession there is no necessity for suit, but in either case if there is any surplus remaining of the proceeds of the sale after the mortgage debt is satisfied, such surplus must be returned to the mortgagor.

LIMITATIONS ON MORTGAGE.—Chattel mortgages, as they are understood in our modern law, have been confined to certain classes of personal property, which are enumerated by statute.

So far as the parties are concerned, one may mortgage to another anything he may choose, but as against creditors a mortgagee will only be protected when he holds a mortgage upon property such as is especially provided for by statute.

These articles are quite numerous, and are frequently changed or added to by our lawmakers, hence we do not give a list of such articles, but recommend the student who wishes to execute a chattel mortgage to consult a reliable attorney.

TEST QUESTIONS.

1. A street railway company purchased a cable rope from the manufacturer with the understanding that it was to be returned if unsatisfactory. The cable company returned the rope. In a suit for the price of the rope by the manufacturer against the railway company, in whose favor should the case be decided?

2. A farmer brings a small sack of wheat as a sample to a dealer. The dealer offers a certain price which the farmer agrees to accept. He leaves the sample and departs. He afterwards sells the grain to a different dealer. Has the first dealer any remedy?

3. Suppose in the above case the grain when offered for delivery proved to be lighter in weight in proportion to the quantity than the sample. Discuss the question of breach of warranty.

4. In a sale of goods to arrive, under the warranty that they should arrive, it was found upon arrival that they were totally unfit for the purpose for which they were sold. Has the buyer any remedy?

5. A signs a mortgage in favor of B, but it is neither acknowledged nor recorded. B, however, holds the mortgage and when due, requests payment. A refuses to pay and says that he did not sign it. Can his signature be proven in any way so as to make him liable?

6. A mortgage is properly made out, signed, and acknowledged, but before it is recorded a creditor of the mortgagor attaches the property. Can he hold it against the mortgage?

CHAPTER XXV.

BAILMENTS.

DEFINITION.—In case of a sale of personal property the ownership is transferred. A bailment, however, contemplates a change of possession without change of ownership.

The subject is so broad that it is difficult to confine it within the bounds of a definition, but the following will be sufficiently comprehensive for our purpose:

"A bailment is a delivery of some chattel by one party to another to be held according to the special purpose of the delivery, and to be returned when that special purpose is accomplished."

The party who delivers the chattel is called the bailor, and the party to whom the delivery is made is called the bailee.

DILIGENCE REQUIRED OF THE BAILEE.—It will be readily understood that a person who has in his charge property belonging to another must exercise some degree of care in its keeping, and the law has endeavored to define the degree of care required under different circumstances.

It is to be noticed first that there are three kinds of bailments with respect to the purpose thereof:

(1) Bailments for the benefit of the bailor only;

(2) For the benefit of both;

(3) For the benefit of the bailee.

In bailments for the bailor's sole benefit, as where A requests another, without compensation, to hold his horse for a few minutes, the diligence required of the other is but slight, and he will not be chargeable for any injury happening to the animal unless he is extremely careless in his holding of the horse.

(134)

Suppose, however, that A gives B a sum of money for holding the horse. This is a mutual benefit. A has his horse taken care of, and B has the money. Here the law requires B to use ordinary care, and if through the lack of ordinary care the horse is injured, B is liable.

Suppose again that B borrows the horse from A for use, not paying any consideration; B is then required to use great diligence in the care of the horse, as the bailment is for his own benefit exclusively.

DEGREES OF NEGLIGENCE.—Corresponding to these degrees of care we have degrees of negligence used in inverse order: thus, great, ordinary, and slight negligence.

In the first example above, B is liable for great negligence only. In the second case he is liable if he is ordinarily negligent. In the third case he is liable if he is only slightly negligent.

The following tabulation will show this relation at a glance:

For benefit of	Care required by bailee	For what negligence liable
Bailor	Slight	Great
Both	Ordinary	Ordinary
Bailee	Great	Slight

This is the general rule in regard to bailments. An exception is "common carriers," which subject will be discussed later.

STANDARD OF DILIGENCE.—While the law uses the words "slight, ordinary, and great" in the attempt to fix a liability in the case of bailments, it will be readily seen that this standard is a most variable and uncertain one.

What would be ordinary care in regard to one transaction, might be the grossest negligence in regard to another.

We will, therefore, take up different kinds of bailments, and illustrate how these degrees are applied.

DEPOSIT.—A deposit may be voluntary or involuntary, and for safe-keeping or for exchange.

A voluntary deposit is made by one giving to another, with his consent, the possession of personal property to keep for the benefit of the former, or of a third party. The person giving is called the depositor, and the person receiving the depositary.

An involuntary deposit is made:

(1) By the accidental leaving or placing of personal property in the possession of any person, without negligence on the part of its owner; or,

(2) In cases of fire, shipwreck, inundation, insurrection, riot, or like extraordinary emergencies, by the owner of personal property committing it, out of necessity, to the care of any person.

Bailments of this class, if without compensation, are for the benefit of the bailor only, and under the rule the bailee is only required to exercise slight diligence, and is liable only in case of great negligence.

Suppose A deposited a sack of coal with B. B would only be required to place it in an out-house; while if A deposited a diamond with B, slight diligence would require that it be placed in a much more secure place.

LOST PROPERTY.—A person who finds property is not required to take charge of it; but if he does so, he may claim compensation for all expense of keeping it, and a reasonable reward in addition thereto.

Finding is therefore a bailment for the benefit of both parties, and the finder must use ordinary diligence in the care of the property.

USE OF PROPERTY.—When property is placed on deposit, the bailee has no right to use the property in any way, unless the proper care of the property necessarily includes its use; as in deposit of a horse, the horse should be exercised for his proper care, but such use must stop at the point where it ceases to benefit the animal.

RETURNING PROPERTY.—A depositary must deliver the thing to the person for whose benefit it was deposited, on demand, whether the deposit was made for a specified time or not, provided his proper charges of keeping, if any, are paid or offered.

He must also return any natural increase of the property at the same time; e. g., if he is given one hundred sheep on deposit, he must return not only the original one hundred sheep, but all others by natural increase which he may have when demand is made.

The property must be returned in as good condition as the degree of care required and the natural deterioration by lapse of time will permit.

LOAN.—A loan for use is a contract by which one gives to another the temporary possession and use of personal property, and the other agrees to return the same thing to him at a future time without reward for its use.

This loan for use, of course, does not transfer the title, and any increase there may be during the period of the loan must be returned to the lender.

A borrower being a bailee for his own benefit, must use great care of the thing lent, and is correspondingly liable for any slight negligence.

In such case the borrower is bound to use as much skill in the care of the thing lent as he causes the lender to believe him to possess; e. g., if he borrows a horse to drive, telling the lender that he is a skilful driver and understands thoroughly the care of horses, when in fact he knows nothing of horses or of driving, he is liable for damage to the horse if caused by his inexperience, no matter how much effort he makes to use the animal properly.

A borrower must repair all injuries to the thing lent, occasioned by his negligence, however slight, though he is not responsible for inevitable accident or "act of God," as the killing of a horse by lightning.

He must not use an article for any purpose other than that for which it was borrowed, and must not relend it to another.

The lender of a thing for use may at any time require its return, even though he lent it for a specified time or purpose, but if the borrower thereby suffers injury, the lender must indemnify him for such loss.

The borrower must return the article without demand when the time has expired, or the purpose is accomplished.

PLEDGE.—A pledge is a deposit of personal property by way of security for the performance of another act. This is a kind of bailment in which each party, the bailor and the bailee, receives a benefit, the bailor receiving some consideration for the pledge, and the bailee holding the pledge as security for something which he has given.

Anything which is capable of delivery may be pledged, and in order to make a valid pledge the property must be actually delivered into the possession of, or placed under the control of, the pledgee.

The degree of care required of the pledgee being ordinary, the pledgee is liable for any ordinary negligence.

He is not liable for slight negligence, hence, under the same circumstances a pledgee can use the thing in his possession with less care than a borrower, and still not be liable for any damage incurred; as in the case of the borrower, it depends a good deal on the nature of the property pledged, and his own representations as to his qualifications and facilities for taking care of the article.

For instance, in the pledge of a horse, if he represents to the pledgor that he understands horses and has a good barn, and other conveniences for the proper care of the animal, when in fact he has neither skill nor accommodations, he will be guilty of ordinary negligence in case the horse suffers from the lack of ordinary care and shelter.

As in the case of property loaned or placed on deposit, the increase of the property pledged must be returned with the property; and it is also a rule of law that the increase, if any, becomes a part of the pledge, and is considered as pledged with the original property.

DISTINGUISHED FROM MORTGAGE.—A pledge of personal property and a mortgage of personal property are alike in that they are both given as security for the performance of some act; but they are radically different in that while the pledged property is actually given into the possession or control of the pledgee, in the case of the mortgage, the mortgaged property is not given into the possession or control of the mortgagee, but the lien on the property is evidenced by a writing called the "mortgage."

SALE OF PLEDGE.—When performance of the act for which a pledge is given as security is due, the pledgee may collect what is due by sale of the pledged property.

Before he can sell, however, he must

(1) Make demand on the pledgor for performance of his obligation.

(2) If performance is refused, the pledgee must give reasonable notice to the pledgor of the time and place of the sale.

(3) A sale must be by public auction.

If the pledgor demands that the pledge be sold even before the obligation is due, the pledgee must sell the article if it can be sold for a price sufficient to satisfy his claim.

If the price received, less the expenses of the sale, is more than enough to pay the debt, the pledgee must pay the surplus to the pledgor.

The pledgee has no right to consider the debt canceled and retain the pledged property in payment. He must sell.

HIRING.—Hiring is a bailment by which one gives to another the temporary possession and use of property for reward. This being a bailment for the benefit of both parties requires ordinary care on the part of the bailee, and he is liable for ordinary negligence, and, as we have previously illustrated, what is ordinary care depends upon the circumstances in each case.

The bailee must repair all injuries or deteriorations caused by his ordinary negligence.

When a thing is hired for a particular purpose, the hirer must not use it for any other purpose, and if he does, the letter may hold him responsible for its safety during such use in all events, and may terminate the hiring; so that the rule of ordinary diligence only applies where the bailee uses the thing for the particular purpose; e. g., suppose A hires a horse to drive to Lodi. Instead of driving to Lodi he drives in an opposite direction. The horse falls through a bridge and is killed without any fault of A. He is nevertheless liable for the loss of the horse because he violated the provisions of his contract of hiring.

The hirer is not liable for any repairs or damage caused by ordinary wear and tear, or such as would ordinarily happen whether the hiring was had or not.

As in the example above, suppose that in driving the horse in a proper manner a shoe was lost, the hirer would not be liable to pay for having the horse shod, and in fact, if necessary to save the horse from lameness, it is the hirer's duty to have the horse shod at the nearest shop, and he may deduct the price from the amount of his hiring.

HIRE OF SERVICES.—This is a delivery of goods to another for the purpose of having some work or service done or performed upon them, for which compensation is to be paid.

It is a bailment for the benefit of both bailor and bailee, and the rule of ordinary diligence and liability for ordinary negligence applies to its full extent.

In arriving at what is ordinary diligence, however, in this bailment perhaps more than in any other, the character of the services to be performed must be carefully considered.

SKILL REQUIRED.—Ordinary care in such a case consists in the handling of the article with such care as ordinarily skilful workmen in that particular line bestow on work of like nature.

EXAMPLE.—A jeweler in repairing a watch, is only required to be an ordinarily good watchmaker in order to escape liability. If he is not an ordinarily good workman in that line it makes no difference how hard he may try to perform the work properly, he is liable if he does not do it as well as an ordinarily skilful watchmaker would perform the work.

A watchmaker or diamond cutter is held to no greater degree of care in his line of work than a street contractor who gravels streets.

The mere fact that there may be more men who can properly gravel streets than there are who can repair watches or cut diamonds, makes no difference in the degree of care required in the services performed.

"Care" should be distinguished from "skill." A diamond setter requires a higher degree of skill and training in order to be ordinarily proficient in his business than a street contractor, but the degree of care is the same.

BAILOR'S INSTRUCTIONS.—If a bailor gives the workman particular instructions as to how to perform certain work upon the article, and the workman endeavors to prosecute the work under these instructions and the article is damaged or destroyed, he is not liable in damages, unless he is grossly negligent.

On the other hand, if the workman deviates from his instructions in a material particular, and the article is thereby damaged, he is liable for all loss.

LIEN.—A person who alters or repairs any article of personal property at the request of the owner, has a lien upon it for his reasonable charges for work done and materials furnished, and may retain possession of the article until such charges are paid, and if the charges are not paid within two months after the owner is notified that the work is done, the bailee may proceed to sell the property at public auction, after notice given, and apply the proceeds of the sale to his charges and costs, giving the remainder, if any, to the owner.

COMMISSION is a contract of bailment by which the bailee undertakes without pay to do some act for the bailor. This being for the bailor's benefit exclusively the bailee is only required to exercise slight diligence, and is liable for damage only in case he is guilty of great negligence; *e. g.*, A is going to a store for groceries, and his neighbor requests him to bring him a sack of flour. This is a commission, and A is not responsible for the loss of the sack of flour unless it occurred through his great negligence.

Such transactions are commonly called "running errands." Commission differs from hire of services only in the matter of compensation and liability incurred.

HIRE OF CUSTODY.—This is a class of bailments in which there is no service to be performed, but simply proper care, and keeping the property from harm, and, as in like cases for the benefit of both parties, ordinary care is required, and the bailee is liable for ordinary negligence.

Under this class may be noted innkeepers, commission merchants, warehousemen, and agistors, those who take in domestic animals for pasturage.

These have been treated generally under the head of "Deposit."

In all of the above-mentioned where goods are left in custody for hire, the bailee must use ordinary care, and is liable for ordinary negligence.

INNKEEPERS.—The term "innkeeper" includes hotel keepers, board and lodging house keepers,

As has been stated they are liable only for ordinary negligence, and the law has made some special provisions applicable to the peculiar character of their business, and affecting their liability.

If the innkeeper keeps a fire-proof safe and notifies his guests that he keeps such a safe, and that he will not be liable for articles of great value and small compass, such as money and jewelry, unless placed therein, he may thus excuse himself, unless he contributes to such loss himself, such as by unlocking the door of the guest's room and leaving it open.

GUESTS.—A guest is any proper person who applies for entertainment and offers to pay for the same.

It may be seen from a careful consideration of the above definition, that an innkeeper is not required to receive drunken, insane, or disreputable people, or those afflicted with contagious diseases, or those who would injure his business in any way; and he may demand pay in advance.

He must receive guests at any hour of the day or night, and if he refuses to do so he is not only liable to the injured party for any damage he may suffer, but is also guilty of a misdemeanor and can be punished criminally.

On the other hand, a guest who obtains board and lodging at an inn, without paying therefor, or who absconds without paying, is guilty of a misdemeanor.

LIEN.—Innkeepers have a lien upon the baggage and other personal property of their guests for their proper charges, and may retain possession of such property. If it remains unclaimed for a period of six months, he may sell the property at public auction, and if there be any surplus after paying his charges and the costs of sale, it must be returned to the owner of the property.

TEST QUESTIONS.

1. Name three kinds of bailments, and the degree of diligence and negligence corresponding to each.

2. A delivers a valuable race horse to B for safe keeping, under the agreement that B may have the use of him in return for his care and feed. B puts the horse into a plow team and works him in an ordinarily careful manner. The horse, however, is so injured as to unfit him for racing purposes. Discuss the right of A to recover damages.

3. A borrows a wheelbarrow. While in his possession it is consumed by fire. Discuss his liability for its loss.

4. A leaves a valise containing valuable articles in B's store, without compensation to B. A thief enters in A's absence and steals the valise. Illustrate under what circumstances B would or would not be liable for the loss.

5. A man demands accommodation at a hotel. He seems in every way a desirable guest, but a large number of the other guests threaten to leave the hotel on account of their personal dislike of this guest. Would the landlord be justified in refusing him accommodation?

6. A pledges a flock of sheep to B. B keeps them for a year, and shears the wool from them at proper times. He returns them with the same amount of wool on the sheep as there was when he received them, but keeps the wool he has shorn off. Will the law protect him in so doing?

7. A wishes to pledge one hundred sacks of wheat in a warehouse. He endorses the warehouse receipt to B as security. Is this such a delivery of the wheat to B as will constitute a pledge?

CHAPTER XXVI.

COMMON CARRIERS.

DEFINITION.—Every one who offers to the public to carry persons, property, or messages, as a business and for hire (except telegraphic and telephonic messages), is a common carrier of whatever he thus offers to carry.

Railroad, steamboat, and stage companies are common carriers of freight and passengers, as well as expressmen, hackmen, draymen, and others who offer as a business to carry goods or passengers for hire.

CARRIERS OF FREIGHT.—A common carrier must, if able to do so, accept and carry whatever is offered to him at a reasonable time and place of a kind that he undertakes or is accustomed to carry, and must not give preference in time, price, or otherwise to one person over another.

He may demand his pay in advance, however, and may refuse to carry unless it is forthcoming.

The obligation resting upon a common carrier being to accept only such kind of freight as he undertakes or is accustomed to carry, an expressman could not be compelled to carry heavy iron or bridge timbers upon his wagon, that not being in the line of his business.

The rule that the carrier must not give preference in price is made to protect the public, and not the carrier, so that it is held that while a carrier can not charge one person a higher rate than what is usual or reasonable, still he may carry for another person at a lower rate than what is reasonable, or without compensation,

(145)

if he chooses; and a further exception to the rule is, that he must always give preference in time to the United States or to a state.

A common carrier must start at such time and place as he announces to the public, unless detained by accident or the elements, or in order to connect with carriers on other lines of travel.

LIABILITY.—Common carriers carrying goods for compensation would, under the general law of liability, be liable only for ordinary negligence, but owing to the extensive and important interest affected by the business of common carriers and the great injury to the public in general where there is any negligence upon the part of the carrier, in the course of the business of carriage, the law has applied a very strict rule to the Common Carrier.

It is this: "A common carrier is absolutely liable for the safety and proper carriage of freight without regard to any degrees of care or negligence."

He is made an *insurer* of the goods confided to his care. To this general rule, however, there are these exceptions.

He is not liable for loss or damage caused by

(1) An inherent defect or spontaneous action of the property itself.

(2) The act of a public enemy.

(3) The act of the law; or

(4) Any irresistible, superhuman cause.

Thus, if fruit is given him which must necessarily spoil before it could reach its destination, he is relieved of liability, or if the carriage is stopped and the goods taken by a Spanish army; or where the laws of the State forbid the sale of such goods, and they are seized by an officer; or where the carriage is struck by lightning and the goods thereby destroyed.

LIMITATION ON LIABILITY.—The obligations of a common carrier can not be limited by general notice on his part, but may be limited by special contract.

Any limitation, however, whether by contract or not, unless

manifested by the signature of the shipper, must be public, lawful, uniform, and reasonable, otherwise it is void.

The following are common limitations which are allowable:

A carrier may print upon his tickets, shipping receipts, or other like documents, specifying the rate of charge, that he will not be liable for damage to breakable articles, unless properly packed; that he will not carry high explosive substances; or that he will not be liable for loss of articles of small compass and great value, unless he is informed at the time of their receipt of the value thereof. These are all reasonable limitations and are held to be lawful.

COMPENSATION.—At all times it has been held that the carrier is entitled to a reasonable compensation. However, as the word "reasonable" is a very elastic term, the modern statutes provide that common carriers shall not charge more than a certain fixed rate, under penalty if they do so. He, of course, is at liberty to charge less than the established rate, should he so desire.

DELIVERY.—What constitutes delivery is as important a question in the case of delivery by a common carrier, as it is in the case of a sale of personal property, and there is a great deal of law upon the subject.

A general statement of the law, however, is about as follows: "A delivery is complete when the goods are placed in the possession of the consignee, or are placed in such a position that he is enabled to take possession at any time."

Thus, it is held that for the purpose of fixing the time when the goods are delivered, a railway company may, after the arrival of certain goods at the station, notify the consignee that the goods have arrived and that after thirty-six hours, or other reasonable time, from the time of notice, the goods will be held by the carrier as the agent of the consignee, and as a warehouseman, and not as carrier.

This applies particularly where it is not the custom or business of the carrier to deliver goods at the residence or place of business of the consignee.

Where, however, it is customary, as is often the case with stage and express·companies, for delivery to be made at the residence or place of business of the consignee, the carrier is liable as a carrier, until he so delivers the goods.

It is to be noted that when the carrier ceases to be a carrier and becomes a warehouseman, as stated above, he is then liable only for ordinary care and ordinary negligence.

If a common carrier accepts freight for a place beyond his usual route he must, unless he stipulates otherwise, deliver it at the end of his route to some other competent carrier for forwarding; and his liability ceases upon such delivery.

The carrier has a lien on the goods in his custody until all his proper charges are made, and may refuse to deliver until the charges are paid.

INTERSTATE COMMERCE LAW.—As the railroad companies are the most important of common carriers in some respects, and as single companies operate their lines of railway through many different states, the Congress of the United States has enacted a law to regulate traffic by common carriers, between states, known as the Interstate Commerce Law.

It is intended to be uniform in its application. Its provisions are in general designed to protect shippers from exorbitant prices, and insure the safe carriage of their property.

The following are a few of its more important provisions:

(1) The provisions of this act shall apply to all common carriers, contracting to carry from one state or territory to another, or through other states and territories to a foreign country, or from foreign countries to any state of the United States, but does not apply to transportation wholly within one state.

(2) All charges must be just and reasonable, and no discriminations made between large or small shippers, or regular and

irregular shippers; no greater charges proportionately for a "short haul" than a "long haul," under similar circumstances, must be made.

(3) A carrier must post conspicuous schedules of rates in every depot, station, or office where passengers or freight are received for transportation, and such published rates must not be deviated from unless ten days' public notice be given of advance in rates. All such rates or schedules must be filed with the United States Commerce Commissioner, and in case of unlawful deviations an injunction may be issued to compel obedience to the law.

(4) The Commissioner has power to inspect and is required to inspect the books of all such carriers, and make reports yearly to the Secretary of the Interior and to Congress.

A CARRIER OF PERSONS for reward must use the utmost care and diligence for their safe carriage, and is not excused for default in this respect by any degree of care.

From the above statement we understand that the carrier of passengers is under the same liability as a carrier of freight, and is, like him, an exception to the general rules of liability.

A carrier of persons for reward then is absolutely liable for any accident which may happen to his passengers, unless caused by their negligence or some irresistible cause which the carrier could not have foreseen and guarded against, such as a stroke of lightning killing a passenger, or the attack of a public enemy.

The law is very strict and goes to extreme lengths in this matter, as it should do in protecting the lives of the public. Thus: "A carrier must not overcrowd or overload the vehicle, and must give all passengers such accommodations as are usual and reasonable; must travel at a reasonable rate of speed without unreasonable delay or deviation," and other similar provisions regulate the conduct of the carrier's business.

It is presumed in this discussion that we are dealing with common carriers of passengers *for reward*. A carrier of persons without reward is only required to use ordinary care and diligence for their safety.

RIGHTS AND DUTIES.—A carrier has a right to enforce such regulations in regard to the conduct of his business as are lawful, public, uniform, and reasonable.

Thus, he may require the fare to be paid in advance, and also that each passenger must purchase a ticket before entering the carriage, and if he fails to do so, may require him to pay ten per cent additional after he boards the carriage.

If a passenger refuses to pay his fare or surrender his ticket on request, the employees of the carrier may put him and his baggage out of the carriage, using no unnecessary force, at any usual stopping place, or near any dwelling house on stopping the carriage.

"Usual stopping place" means a regular station where people reside. A water tank at which a train usually stopped for water, was held nevertheless not to be a usual stopping place under this provision.

A passenger if ejected at a usual stopping place, may re-enter on offering to pay his fare from the place he originally boarded the carriage, or on producing his ticket.

If ejected at a dwelling house, however, he would have no right to re-enter, it not being a place where passengers are received.

WHO ARE PASSENGERS.—Every proper person who tenders the proper fare must be accepted as a passenger by the carrier.

The general statement of the law is practically the same as in the case of an innkeeper, but in the application there is a difference. The innkeeper, it will be remembered, is not required to receive persons afflicted with contagious or infectious diseases, or persons of bad character, or who otherwise would bring disrepute upon his house, or cause a loss of business.

The law presumes that there are places for the care of persons suffering from diseases, and places where persons of bad character may find accommodation, but it does not raise any such presumption in the case of a common carrier.

So far as he is concerned he must accept even persons afflicted with diseases, although he might be required to provide separate apartments for them.

He must not, however, accept drunken and disorderly persons who would be dangerous to the life and limb of other passengers.

He can not refuse to accept any person on account of his bad character or reputation, so long as he conducts himself properly. Neither can he refuse to accept a person because of his blindness or physical deformity.

In some of the southern states, special statutes have been passed requiring railroad companies to provide separate cars for colored persons, and when such cars are so provided, the colored persons can not ride in the same car with white persons.

In California and in the western states generally, there is no such law, and other races, such as the negroes or Chinese, may ride in the same car with white persons, upon complying with the same conditions.

A person who is not lawfully on board the carriage, or who rides in the part not designated for passengers, such as the brake-beam of a car, can not claim any damages in case of injury to their persons, except in case where the employees of the carrier resort to unnecessary force in ejecting him, and thereby injure him; the rule being, as stated above, that the carrier must use no unnecessary force in ejecting any one from the carriage.

CONTRIBUTORY NEGLIGENCE.—As we have seen, a common carrier of persons may make rules for the conduct of his business, and may require passengers to conform to them, if they are:

(1) Lawful;
(2) Public;
(3) Uniform; and
(4) Reasonable.

Under these provisions, a railroad company usually posts notices requiring passengers not to stand on the platform; to keep heads and arms inside of car windows; not to get on or off the train while in motion, etc.

If a person is injured while violating any such regulations as the above, he is said to be guilty of contributory negligence; that is, he contributes to his own injury, and the company is not liable in damages where such negligence on the part of the passenger can be shown.

A passenger is also guilty of contributory negligence if he does any act which contributes to his own injury, even though not in violation of some regulation of the carrier.

He might in a spirit of bravado swing himself from a moving train, and hold only by his hands, or might climb to the top of a car and run along on the top, or do other things which no prudent man would be expected to do, and which the carrier could not possibly provide against by regulations.

In such case, he can claim nothing from the carrier if he is injured. The happening of an injury, however, is prima-facie evidence that the carrier has been negligent, and it devolves upon him to show that the passenger contributed to his own injury. The passenger is bound to exercise ordinary care for his own safety, and if he does not, he relieves the company from liability to the extent that he himself is negligent.

LUGGAGE.—A common carrier of persons, unless his vehicle is fitted for the reception of persons exclusively, must receive and carry a reasonable amount of luggage for each passenger, without charge, except for an excess of weight of over 100 pounds for a passenger, provided that if such carrier be a proprietor of a stage line he need not receive and carry for each passenger, without charge, more than 60 pounds of luggage.

Luggage may consist of whatever the passenger takes with him for his personal use and convenience; hence trunks, valises, bicycles, and tricycles are held to be proper luggage.

A common carrier, while he must carry a great variety of articles under the term luggage, still may limit his liability for loss or damage in a reasonable amount. This is usually fixed at not to exceed $100 for a trunk, or $50 for a valise.

In any event, a carrier of luggage could not be made to pay for the loss of the contents of a valise which were of unusual and extraordinary value, such as a valise full of money or jewelry.

In order to make a carrier liable for loss or damage to luggage it is necessary to give it into his keeping.

If a passenger carries his valise or other baggage with him, he alone is responsible for its safety, unless its loss occurs through negligence of the carrier or his servants.

RIGHTS OF THIRD PARTIES.—Common carriers are, of course, liable generally for any violation of the rights of parties, other than their passengers, the same as any one else.

Railroad companies are the most numerous and powerful of common carriers in this country, and special statutes have been directed toward them.

A railroad company must make and maintain a good and sufficient fence on either or both sides of their track and property, under penalty of damages for any domestic animals killed by their trains.

This, of course, does not apply in cities or towns where stock is not permitted to run about the highways, as in such case the owners of stock would themselves be violators of the law; and "the law will not aid wrong-doers."

Such carriers are further required to ring a bell and blow a whistle at specified distances from each street or road crossing, and are liable for damages for all injuries suffered by third parties when these provisions are violated; and the person in charge of a locomotive engine who fails to so ring the bell, or sound the whistle, is guilty of a misdemeanor and may be punished criminally; and generally, any employee who wilfully omits a duty by which human life is endangered is guilty of a misdemeanor.

A number of cases have arisen in which sparks from a locomotive engine have set fire to grain fields and other personal property along the route of the railway.

The rule of damages deduced from these cases is generally stated as follows:

That a railroad company is liable for all property destroyed by reason of fires from locomotive engines, the law requiring such companies to furnish their locomotive smoke-stacks with such cinder screens as will effectually prevent such destruction of property.

TELEGRAPHS.—Telegraph companies are considered under the head of carriers, but there are some important differences which will be noted.

One great difference is in the matter of liability. A carrier of telegraphic messages is required to use great care and diligence in the transmission and delivery of messages, and is liable for slight negligence, but is not an insurer of the correctness or safety of the transmission as is the case with other carriers.

Such carrier must deliver a message to such place and person as provided in the address, if he is within a distance of two miles from the main office nearest the place of address, and should he delay unreasonably, either in the transmission or delivery, he is liable in damages to the party injured.

ORDER OF TRANSMISSION.—A carrier of messages by telegraph must, if it is practicable, transmit every such message immediately upon its receipt, but if this is not practicable he must transmit them in the following order:

(1) Messages concerning public business;

(2) Messages intended for immediate publication in newspapers;

(3) Messages relating to sickness or death;

(4) Other messages in the order in which they were received.

RIGHTS AND DUTIES.—A carrier of telegraphic messages

may limit his liability in a similar manner as a carrier of passengers or freight.

He may stipulate that he will not be liable above a certain specified sum, unless the message is "repeated," that is, sent back to the sending office for comparison.

He can not, however, absolutely limit his liability to any certain amount, as momentous consequences may follow a wrong dispatch.

He may demand pay in advance, and require senders to write in ink, or on particular sized paper.

He may refuse to pay any damage caused by the missending or misreading of a message written in cipher, unless the cipher is explained to him, cipher messages being those in which signs or letters are used to represent words.

A carrier is liable, however, in any case where damage occurs through a change, by the operator, of the message as written by the sender.

In one case a company was compelled to pay damages where the message read, "Send Shep by next train," and the operator, thinking to correct poor spelling, sent the message thus: "Send sheep by next train," thus causing a dealer to send his agent a large consignment of sheep instead of a dog named Shep, thereby causing great expense and loss to the owner.

If an operator wilfully divulges the contents of a telegraphic message, or alters it unlawfully, the company is not only liable for any damage which may occur in consequence, but the operator is guilty of a felony and may be punished criminally therefor.

TELEPHONES.—The law of telephones is of recent growth, but so far as it has developed, telephones have been generally held to be governed by the same rules as telegraphs, so far as in the nature of things they can be made applicable.

Thus, as in the case of other carriers, telephone companies are bound to give prompt and proper service to all comers, and are liable for damages in case they refuse.

Of course, they can not be held responsible for missent messages as they do not, strictly speaking, send any messages at all, but simply furnish the appliance by which the customer sends his own message. They are liable only for ordinary negligence in the conduct of their business.

TEST QUESTIONS.

1. A passenger on a train refuses to give up his ticket because the train is so crowded that he can not get a seat. The conductor puts him off the train. Can he recover damages?

2. A freight company refuses to take goods because of a strike on the line. Can a shipper recover damages suffered on account of refusal of the company to carry the goods?

3. A railroad company unloads goods at its depot, and the goods are immediately destroyed by fire. Is the company liable for the loss?

4. A car load of live stock consigned to B is killed in a wreck. The wreck is not caused by any negligence of the company. Will the company be liable for the damages?

5. If goods perish on the road by "act of God," does the seller or the buyer bear the loss?

6. A passenger refuses to pay his fare; the train is stopped and he is ejected at a farm house. He then offers to pay his fare, but is refused admittance to the train. May he recover damages?

7. Explain the doctrine of "contributory negligence."

8. A package is sent by express to a grocery store in San Francisco. The package is stolen out of the delivery wagon of the express company. Discuss the liability of the company.

9. While a train is traveling at its customary speed a passenger attempts to pass from one car to another, and in doing so falls from the car and is injured. Discuss his right to collect damages.

10. A writes a telegraphic message and delivers it to the operator. The operator makes a mistake in reading the message as written, which results in loss to A. Discuss A's right to recover damages.

CHAPTER XXVII.

SHIPPING.

GENERAL DEFINITIONS.—The term "ship" or "shipping" includes steamboats, sailing vessels, canal boats, barges, and every structure to be navigated from place to place for the transportation of merchandise or persons.

A charter party is the contract by which a ship is let or hired out to a person for use.

BILL OF LADING.—A bill of lading is an instrument in writing, signed by a carrier or his agent, describing the freight, stating the name of the consignor, the terms of the contract for carriage, and an agreement that the freight will be delivered to a certain person, or order, at a specified place.

As we have stated before, a bill of lading has by special statute, been made a negotiable instrument, and can therefore pass from hand to hand in the same manner and with like effect as is the case with a Bill of Exchange.

Bills of lading are usually signed in sets of three; one being given to the consignor, which operates as a receipt for goods received, another held by the carrier as a memorandum of the transaction, and the third sent to the consignee.

A bill of lading, as used in sending by ship, is practically the same as a bill of lading used in sending goods by train.

LIABILITY OF MARINE CARRIERS.—A marine carrier is liable in like manner as an inland carrier, except for loss or injury caused by perils of the sea or fire.

Perils of the sea are from,

(1) Storms and waves;

(2) Rocks, shoals, or other obstacles;

(3) Change of climate; and

(4) Generally, all dangers peculiar to the sea.

A marine carrier is not liable for damages for loss of goods by fire, unless caused by the design or neglect of the carrier or his agents.

In consequence of the great danger for loss of goods sent by sea, it is customary for all shippers to place insurance on such goods.

MARITIME LOANS.—On long voyages it is not uncommon for a ship to be disabled so as to need repairs beyond the amount of coin or credit which she may have. In such cases the captain of the vessel is authorized to borrow money for the purpose of repairs, and give as security a document in the nature of a mortgage upon the ship or its cargo, or both, for the repayment of the loan.

This document is called a *bottomry bond*, if made on the vessel, and if made on the cargo, is called a *respondentia bond*.

PAYMENT OF LOANS.—It sometimes happens that two or more loans may be required at different ports before the vessel reaches her destination, and in such case, the rule of priority in repayment is exactly the reverse of the rule in ordinary mortgages.

In ordinary mortgages the mortgage first made must be first paid. On marine loans the last made must be first paid, on the theory that the last loan saved the vessel from destruction. These loans being made with the ship and cargo as security, are required to be repaid only in case the ship reaches her destination in safety, and not otherwise.

AUTHORITY OF SHIPMASTER.—A master of a ship is a general agent for its owner, and also general agent for each of the owners of the cargo.

He, therefore, in addition to authority to borrow money as above described, has authority to do whatever the owners might do for the preservation of their respective interests; so in case a cargo, if found to be of such perishable nature, or in such damaged condition that if left on board the ship, would be lost, he has power to sell such cargo; and likewise if the ship is seriously injured beyond the possibility of pursuing the voyage, the master may sell the ship; and in like case he of course may sell the cargo, if no other ship can be obtained to carry it to its destination at reasonable cost.

He likewise has power, in case of storm or other danger which makes it necessary, to throw overboard such part of the cargo as is necessary for the safety of the ship. In such case the owners of the part of the cargo which is saved must contribute their pro rata of the value of the cargo thrown overboard to the owner of such cargo.

This act of contribution is called "General Average."

TEST QUESTIONS.

1. A vessel is delayed on her journey, for repairs. She has on board a cargo of fruit. Under what circumstances would the captain be justified in selling it?

2. Illustrate circumstances under which the master of a vessel would be justified in throwing overboard part of the cargo.

CHAPTER XXVIII.

AGENCY.

DEFINITION.—An agent is one who represents another, called the principal, in dealing with third persons.

Such representation is called "agency." Any person having the capacity to contract, may appoint an agent, and any person may be an agent. The last sentence should be carefully noted.

It will be remembered that persons having capacity to contract are those who are not minors, persons of unsound mind, or persons deprived of civil rights.

Any one of these three classes can not be a principal, but *any* person may be an agent. This includes, of course, even the three classes above excepted, but as a matter of fact of the three classes a person deprived of civil rights could not ordinarily be an agent, as he is usually confined in the State Prison; and a person who is an absolute idiot, would, as a matter of fact, be incapable of attending to business of any kind, and hence could not be an agent.

Minors, however, may be agents to the full extent of the definition.

CLASSES OF AGENTS.—Generally speaking there are two classes of agents, general agents and special agents.

A general agent is one who is empowered to transact all business of his principal of a particular nature, or all business at a particular place.

He may, without special instructions, do any act in regard to the business, which his principal could do if personally present.

A special agent is an agent for a particular act or transaction, and is empowered to do only what is necessary to complete that act or transaction.

APPOINTMENT OF AGENT.—An oral authorization is sufficient for any purpose, except that an authority to enter into a contract, required by law to be in writing, can only be given by an instrument in writing; thus if a person wishes to appoint an agent for the purpose of selling land, or mortgaging property, he must give him such authority in writing, under the same solemnities as is required in the deed or mortgage.

Such an instrument is called a Power of Attorney, and simply sets forth the names of the parties, and the power which the one gives to the other. It is signed by the principal, and must be acknowledged and recorded in order to give proper effect to the agent's subsequent acts.

EVIDENCE OF AUTHORITY.—In dealing with agents, a third party does so at his own peril, and must be able to show that he had reasonable grounds for believing the agent to be possessed of proper authority.

A written authorization, signed by the principal, is of course good evidence.

In case there is no written authority, the fact that a principal has allowed another to hold himself out as his agent, and by his conduct has assented to his transactions, is good evidence of the creation of the agency.

An office clerk or bookkeeper might be held to have power to collect bills for the firm, although that was not his exclusive business; and where a servant is repeatedly sent to a store for goods on credit the merchant is justified in extending reasonable credit, and the master is responsible for all such goods bought, even though in some cases the master did not authorize their purchase.

IMPLIED POWERS.—As a general rule an agent, even though he is a special agent, has implied power to do all acts which necessarily pertain to the carrying out of the purposes of the agency.

Thus, an authority to sell property includes authority to warrant the title of the principal, and to warrant the quality and quantity of the property.

A general agent to sell, who is intrusted by the principal with the possession of the thing sold, has authority to receive the price at any time until his agency is revoked; and even a special agent to sell has authority to receive the price on delivery of the thing sold, but not afterwards, as his agency. is, of course, terminated with the closing of the sale.

So an agent to sell has power to incur proper charges for carriage or expressage in delivering the property.

LIABILITY OF PARTIES.—There being three parties to a transaction where an agent is employed, instead of two, as in contracts previously discussed, there arise many questions as to the liability in case of pecuniary loss resulting from the transaction, and the law has prescribed certain rules governing the varying conditions under which loss may occur.

LIABILITY OF PRINCIPAL TO THIRD PARTIES.—"A principal is responsible for all acts of his agent done within the *apparent* scope of the agent's authority." This rule must be carefully examined and understood.

The word "apparent" is very important in its signification. A may employ an agent for the purpose of buying general hardware. He may not choose to purchase stoves, yet if his agent, being known as his agent for the purchase of general hardware, does purchase stoves, the stove manufacturers may recover damages from A in case of his refusal to receive or pay for the stoves.

The principal is thus liable for whatever acts the agent does which appear to be within the scope of his authority, and he can not bind third parties by any private instructions given to the agent without the knowledge of the third party.

AGENTS WRONGFUL ACTS.—A principal is responsible to third persons for the negligence of his agent in the transaction of the business of the agency, including wrongful acts committed by such agent in and as a part of the transaction of the business.

For example: While it is the duty of an engineer to stop a train, still if he does so suddenly and without just reason therefor, and thereby injures passengers, the railroad company is liable in damages; or in case of a bridge, if the builder's agent negligently and improperly constructed it so that accidents are caused thereby, the builder is liable.

An agent who thus wilfully commits a wrong may also be held liable criminally if his intent can be shown to injure life or limb; and as a matter of course the agent's wilful acts, which are not done in and as part of the business of the agency, are chargeable only to himself; as in case of the engineer, if while in charge of the employer's engine, he should shoot a man, the principal could not in such case be held liable, shooting not being a part of the agency.

So a principal is liable for the unskilfulness of his agent. If a stage company employs an unskilful driver who overturns the coach and maims passengers, the company is liable, and can not excuse themselves by saying he was recommended as a skilful driver, or by any like excuse.

The principal is bound to employ proper agents in dealing with third persons.

PRINCIPAL'S LIABILITY BY RATIFICATION. — It sometimes happens that an agent will do an act beyond both the actual and apparent scope of his authority. In such cases the principal may afterwards agree to ratify, or be bound by the act, and when he does so, he is liable for all damage which may arise in consequence of the act.

Ratification may be manifested,

(1) By actual notice to the third party by the principal;

(2) By accepting the benefits of the act;

(3) By neglecting to disaffirm within a reasonable time after notice of the act.

A principal can not ratify an act which he had no power to authorize beforehand; and if he ratifies part of an indivisible transaction, it is a ratification of the whole.

Thus, if he accepts goods purchased without authority, he can not refuse to pay the price. Where an authority is required to be in writing a ratification can only be made by a similar writing.

LIABILITY OF AGENT.—The principal is, of course, liable to the agent on his contract of employment for payment of the agent's salary, and for all proper expenses which the agent may incur in carrying out the principal's instructions.

The principal is also liable for any damage which may happen to the agent, without the agent's fault, in carrying out the instructions of the principal.

This latter rule has occasioned much litigation. It must be accepted with some qualification and explanation. For instance, a principal directs his agent to operate a certain piece of machinery. If the agent asserts that he is a skilful operator, and familiar with that particular machine, when in fact he is not, and is injured because of his lack of knowledge, the principal can not be held liable.

On the other hand, if the agent is known to be ignorant of the machinery, and the principal gives certain instructions which the agent follows to the best of his ability, using ordinary care, and is then injured, the principal is liable for damages for the injury; so also the principal is liable to an agent for damages for injuries received by reason of defective machinery or tools supplied to the workman by the principal.

AGENT'S LIABILITY TO THIRD PARTIES.—One who assumes to act as an agent is responsible to a third person and to the principal for his acts in the course of his agency, in the following cases:

(1) When credit is given to him personally;

(2) When he enters into a written contract in the name of his principal without believing that he has authority to do so;

(3) When his acts are wrongful in their nature.

Of course, when credit is given to him personally he becomes to that extent the principal in the transaction, and in such cases is personally liable. ·

Under the second subdivision both he and the principal are liable under the written contract to third parties.

When his acts are wrongful in their nature, he, as a matter of right, should be and is held responsible; and as we have seen, when such wrongful acts are connected with the business of the agency, and as a part of such agency, the principal is also responsible.

The agent can not claim in order to relieve himself of liability for a wrongful act, that he did it under authority of the principal, as a principal can not give an authority to commit a wrong; any such attempted authority is absolutely void, and the agent is not liable as an agent, but as a wrong-doer.

LIABILITY TO PRINCIPAL.—An agent is generally liable to the principal for all acts which he may do in the name of the principal, but without the scope of his actual authority.

It is his duty to obey strictly the instructions of the principal.

In only one case has he power to disobey the principal's instructions, and that is in a case where it is clearly in the interests of his principal that he should do so, and there is not time to communicate with the principal.

The most familiar instance under this doctrine, is the case of a master of a ship, who in emergency may not only hypothecate the ship and cargo, but even sell both, or cast the cargo overboard. Such acts must not be done, and the agent will be liable therefor, unless he can show an overwhelming necessity for such disobedience to instructions.

An agent is bound to disclose all information which he may obtain, to the principal, and must not in any way advance his own interests at the expense of the interests of his principal; e. g.,

A may instruct his agent to sell wheat if he can get $1.50 per cental. The agent receives $1.60 per cental. He has no right to appropriate the difference to his own use; on the contrary, should he disobey instructions and sell the wheat for $1.40 per cental, he must bear the loss.

The principal is entitled to the highest degree of skill possessed by the agent in the line of his employment, and he is liable to the principal for any loss resulting from his lack of proper attention to the business of the agency.

RIGHTS AND DUTIES OF THIRD PARTIES.—A third party in dealing with an agent is bound to exercise ordinary care and prudence in learning the extent of the agent's authority, and if he is deceived through lack of ordinary prudence, the principal can not be made to respond in damages.

He is not, however, bound to make a special investigation into the details of the agency before transacting business with the agent.

Thus, where even a stranger presents himself, representing that he is a selling agent of some well-known business house, and carries with him certain samples, and generally conducts himself and presents such credentials as men in his class of business usually present, a purchaser would be justified in giving an order to such person and holding the principal responsible for a failure to fill such order.

NOTICE TO AGENT.—As against principal, both principal and agent are deemed to have notice of what either has notice of, and in good faith and the exercise of ordinary care and diligence should communicate to the other. Hence, if a third person desires to change or countermand an order when it is proper to do so, he may send notice to the agent of his desire, and such notice will be deemed to be notice to the principal.

AGENCY TERMINATED.—An agency may be terminated, generally speaking, in three ways:

(1) By expiration of time;

(2) Act of the parties;

(3) Change in condition of the parties, or subject matter.

BY EXPIRATION OF TIME.—An agent may be hired for a specified time, and at the expiration of that time his agency is terminated, unless by his contract he is also required to finish certain work. In such case the time is extended until such work is finished; and in case no time is set, a special agency is terminated as soon as the particular business for which the agent was appointed, is consummated.

ACT OF PARTIES.—The principal may at any time revoke the agency by giving proper notice to the agent, and to third parties dealing through him, unless the agent's power is coupled with an interest in the subject matter, as in case he is part owner of the business.

The agent also may renounce the agency at any time upon notice, but he is liable for any damages which may occur by his leaving the employment before the expiration of his term, or before the finishing of his special work.

In any case no particular form of notice, either by the agent or his principal, is required. Any notice which will properly inform either of the desire of the other, is sufficient.

CHANGE IN CONDITION OF THE PARTIES AND IN SUBJECT MATTER.—The agency is revoked by the incapacity or death of either party, though in case of the death or incapacity of the principal, the agent is bound to exercise his powers as agent for a reasonable time if necessary to preserve the property of his principal, and is entitled to compensation for such service.

Bankruptcy of either party is such a change in the condition of the parties as terminates the agency. If the principal becomes bankrupt, his property is all placed out of his control, and his authority terminates.

By the bankruptcy of the agent, he is technically considered to have lost his business standing for the time; but it seems there is no objection to a person's being employed as an agent while his property is in the hands of a court of bankruptcy.

The extinction of the subject of the agency, such as the death of a horse, which an agent was employed to train, or the decaying of fruit which the agent was employed to sell, terminates the agency.

TEST QUESTIONS.

1. An agent makes a contract with B, a third party, in his own name. B does not know of the agency. Can the principal enforce this contract with B?

2. In the above case should B discover the real principal, can he enforce a claim for damages against him?

3. An agent to sell goods, buys certain goods for his firm. Discuss the obligations of his firm to pay for the goods.

4. A has authority as a general agent; he is given special instructions in regard to the business. Can he violate the special instructions and escape liability on the ground of being a general agent?

5. A, as an agent, sold a sewing machine to B at an agreed price of $30. After the machine was delivered the company demanded payment in the sum of $50 for the machine. Which price must B pay?

6. A, who is an experienced man in that line, is employed to "run" a threshing machine. His foot is crushed in the machinery. Discuss his right to recover damages from the owners.

7. Farmer Smith's workhand, while burning stubble, negligently allowed the fire to extend to Farmer B's land, and B's house is burned. Who is liable?

8. In the above question would it alter the case if the farmhand wilfully directed the fire toward B's house so that it was consumed?

CHAPTER XXIX.

PARTNERSHIP.

DEFINITION.—Partnership is the association of two or more persons for the purpose of carrying on business together and dividing its profits, and sharing its losses between them.

Partnerships may be either General or Special, and formed by either,

(1) A written contract;

(2) An oral agreement; or

(3) By implication.

In any case, a partnership can be formed only by the consent of all the parties thereto, and therefore no new partner can be admitted into the firm without the consent of every member thereof.

WHEN IS A PARTNERSHIP FORMED.—The best evidence of the formation of a partnership is a written contract which has been entered into by the parties. Such a contract, called "Articles of Co-partnership," is usually a formal document setting forth the names of the parties, the kind of business, the amount of capital contributed by each; and generally, such agreements as they may wish.

When oral contracts are made, it is sometimes difficult to determine whether the contract is one of partnership or of agency, especially if one person does all of the work, the other furnishing all of the money or other capital; and in cases of partnership by implication, the acts of the parties alone can be depended upon to determine whether or not a partnership exists.

EXAMPLES.—A owns land; he enters into a contract with

(170)

B to farm that land, and deliver to him one-third of the products. This is held not to be a partnership, but a mere leasing; while two persons engaging in the farming of land and raising of wheat together, with the understanding that the product was to be divided proportionately, the contract was held to constitute a partnership; and it is held as a general rule that where a person receives a certain per cent of the profits as profits, he is a partner; but where he receives merely a sum of money equal to a certain per cent of the profits, he is not a partner.

LIABILITY OF PARTNERS.—Each member of a partnership, by entering into such partnership, makes himself liable for all of the debts, if any there be, against the partnership.

It matters not that he may own but a small interest in the business, he is liable nevertheless for all debts to whatever extent, and his personal property may be taken and sold for partnership debts if necessary to satisfy them.

This refers, however, only to the usual, or, as it is called, a general partnership. A special partnership is described in the next section.

SPECIAL PARTNERSHIP is a partnership formed under special statute, and may consist of one or more general partners, and one or more special partners.

The chief difference between a general and a special partner is that the special partner may limit his liability for losses by making and recording Articles of Co-partnership, in which is stated the amount of stock or share which he has contributed, and for which he will be liable.

Such certificate of partnership must also be published, so as to give full notice to the public that such partnership is formed.

When the special partners have properly complied with the law in forming the partnership, each special partner can be held liable only for the amount of capital invested.

Thus, if A, as a special partner, invests $5,000, he is only obliged to pay in case of loss $5,000 of indebtedness, while the general partners are each liable as in ordinary co-partnerships for the total indebtedness.

FIRM NAME.—A firm name is often composed simply of the names of the members of the co-partnership, but any designation may be made, and business conducted thereunder, as "The California Hardware Company;" but in case a fictitious name is used, such as "The California Hardware Company," the partners are required to publish in a newspaper, and file a certificate with the County Clerk of the County where the business is conducted, stating the true names in full of the members of the co-partnership, under penalty of being deprived of the right to bring a suit in court until such publication and filing is done.

In the case of a special partnership, it is not lawful to use the name of the special partner in the firm name, unless it be accompanied with the word "limited."

This last provision is for the protection of people who might give extensive credit to the firm on the supposition that the one whose name so appeared was a general partner.

CLASSES OF PARTNERS.—The classes of partners are:

(1) Ostensible;

(2) Dormant;

(3) Nominal; and

(4) Special.

AN OSTENSIBLE OR REAL PARTNER is one who allows his name to be used publicly as a partner, and who is really a partner.

A DORMANT PARTNER, as the word indicates, is a sleeping partner, or one who is hidden, and does not take any active part in the partnership, nor allow his name to appear in any way, so that no one knows that he is a partner except the members of the firm.

The object in concealing his identity as a partner is, of course, to escape liability in case debts are created.

He is, in a sense, a real partner in the firm, and if he is discovered by a creditor, he can be compelled to pay any and all debts of the firm in the same manner as though he had at all times been known as a partner, and it makes no difference that the debt was created during the time that he was dormant.

A NOMINAL PARTNER is, as the name indicates, a partner in name only, and as between the partners themselves has nothing to do with the business, either to share profits or divide losses; however, as the purpose of a nominal partner is for the strengthening of the credit of the firm by use of the name of some responsible man, this man, the nominal partner, must pay the penalty, should any debts or losses occur.

In brief, so far as third parties are concerned he is to all intents and purposes an ostensible or real partner.

SPECIAL PARTNERS have already been discussed in distinguishing between special and general partners.

AUTHORITY OF PARTNERS.—Each partner is a general (as distinguished from special) agent for the firm, and as such general agent he may bind the firm by any and all acts which he may do in the carrying on of the partnership business in the ordinary manner.

Hence, he may buy and sell goods, give warranties, appoint agents, and make, accept, or endorse negotiable papers in the firm name.

The following acts are forbidden him. He can not

(1) Make an assignment of partnership property;

(2) Sell the good-will of the business;

(3) Submit a claim to arbitration;

(4) Generally, do any act which would make it impossible to carry on the ordinary business of the partnership.

A partner in all business transactions relating to the firm business must hold the interests of the firm above his personal interest; hence, he has no right to make a purchase with firm funds, and, should the venture be profitable, appropriate the profits, and if unprofitable, charge the firm with the loss.

It must be either a firm act or an individual act; and as a rule he can not transact any business in opposition to the interest of the firm.

PARTNERSHIP AGREEMENTS.—Any agreement in regard to the nature of the business, amount of stock to be employed, the conduct of the business, or in fact anything pertaining to the partnership, is valid as between the partners themselves, so long as it is lawful; and as between themselves a court of equity will enforce all such agreements, but as against third parties no secret agreements between the partners which work injury to a third party, are valid.

Thus, if A holds himself out as a general partner, while as a matter of fact he has a secret understanding with his partners that he shall be only liable for a small proportion of the debt, he is nevertheless liable as a general partner, and his secret agreement is void, so far as the creditor is concerned, although he may enforce contribution from the others.

Even where a partner acts in bad faith toward another, so long as the agreement is proper and lawful, all of the partners are bound by it, if third parties would be injured by a refusal to abide by the act, but not otherwise.

Of course, in all cases where one partner suffers damage through the act of another, he has his remedy against the other.

PROFITS.—All profits made by a general partner in the course of any business, usually carried on by the partnership, belong to the firm; and should he engage in business adversely to the interests of his firm, or use partnership funds, all profits belong to the partnership.

Partners may agree as to how profits shall be divided. Two men may enter into co-partnership and agree to divide the profits equally, or one may have put in more capital than the other and they may divide it, giving one two-thirds, the other one-third of the profits, or in any way that they may agree upon.

As we have seen, persons may enter into co-partnership without intending, or without really knowing that they are partners, under agreements for the share of profits, but a mere clerk or employee, who is to be paid a commission in proportion to the amount of profits made, is not a partner.

LOSSES.—It is usual for partners to agree among themselves that they each will pay all losses in the same proportion as they divide profits.

This agreement, so far as it concerns the partners, is binding upon them, but as we have noted, can not bind creditors, as the law provides that each partner shall be liable for the entire indebtedness of the firm, unless he has limited his liability, as in the case of a special partnership.

CAPITAL.—The capital of a partnership consists of anything and everything which is used in the conduct of the partnership business.

It may consist of money, merchandise, store fixtures, horses, wagons, hay, or even the services of one of the partners, or the use of a horse and wagon.

It is frequently the case that one partner invests a certain amount of money as his pro rata of the capital, while another contributes his skill, knowledge, and experience in the business as his pro rata.

SUITS.—A general partnership may sue and be sued in the firm name in the same manner as an individual.

In the case of partnerships doing business under a fictitious name they must, as we have seen, file with the County Clerk the true names of the partners before they are allowed to bring suits, while any one wishing to sue the firm, may sue it under the fictitious name, and when the true names of the partners are discovered, they may be inserted in the papers.

DISSOLUTION.—A general partnership is dissolved as to all the partners,

(1) By a lapse of time prescribed by agreement for its duration;

(2) By the expressed will of any partner, if there is no such agreement;

(3) By the death of a partner;

(4) By the transfer to a third party of the interest of any partner;

(5) By a judgment of dissolution.

BY AGREEMENT.—In all cases where articles of co-partnership are formally drawn up, it is customary to state the time for the continuance of such partnership, and when that time elapses any partner may consider the partnership at an end and demand a division of the property.

Of course, if the firm continues to do business after the lapse of such time, it is still a partnership.

Where a partnership is formed for a particular purpose, there is an implied agreement that the partnership shall end when that purpose has been accomplished.

When there is no agreement the partnership may be, as stated above, dissolved by any partner by his simply declaring that he withdraws from the partnership, and demanding an accounting and settlement of the affairs.

BY DEATH.—Partnership is a confidential and personal relation between men. Men combine only with others whom they can trust, or for whom they have a particular liking, or in whose judgment they have confidence.

Hence, when one partner dies, it would be injustice to the other members to allow his heirs to take a part in the conduct of the partnership business without the consent of the others, and the law has declared that the death of one partner dissolves the partnership, and there must be an accounting and a settling up of the business.

TRANSFER TO THIRD PERSONS dissolves a partnership, and for a similar reason, as stated in the last section. A third person entering into the firm might not be a person desired by the remaining members; hence when a sale is had the partnership is dissolved and a new one created, if the business is to be further conducted.

BY JUDGMENT.—A court of equity is seldom called into requisition to dissolve a partnership, unless the partners are unable to agree upon the terms of dissolution.

A general partner, however, is entitled to judgment of dissolution under the following and similar grounds:

(1) When a partner becomes legally incapable of contracting;

(2) When he fails to perform his duties, or is guilty of serious misconduct, such as habitual drunkenness;

(3) When there is a permanent loss in the conduct of the business;

(4) Where there is serious quarreling or contentions among the partners so as to render it impracticable properly to carry on business.

In any of these cases the partner complaining must present in his complaint to the proper court full statements of the facts upon which he seeks to dissolve the partnership. In a proper case, the court may appoint a receiver to settle up the business, and make proper division of the proceeds, if any.

RIGHTS OF THIRD PARTIES.—In the event of a dissolution of the firm, the parties who retire from the firm must give proper notice to all creditors of the fact of dissolution in order to protect themselves from liability.

This notice is usually given by means of an advertisement inserted in a newspaper, and by changing the firm name on the signs and office stationery, and sometimes by sending notices by mail to the creditors of the firm.

A retiring partner is, however, liable at all times for debts incurred while he was a partner in the firm.

12

Creditors may enforce their rights against the capital stock for old debts, even after a new partner has come into the business.

PARTNERS' AUTHORITY AFTER DISSOLUTION.— When a firm has been dissolved, it is customary for one of the partners to settle all outstanding accounts and collect all moneys due the firm, and he is clothed with the power to do all such things, and only such things, as are necessary to properly settle up the business of the partnership.

In case there is a loss, he should apply the proceeds of the partnership property to the settlement of all claims against the firm.

If there is a surplus he should divide it amongst the partners in accordance with the agreement entered into in forming the partnership.

It is only after partnership assets are all exhausted that creditors may hold the members of the firm individually liable for partnership debts.

TEST QUESTIONS.

1. A allows B to farm his land for a year, agreeing to accept as rent one-third of the crop raised. Does this agreement constitute a partnership?
2. The same parties farm the land together, A furnishing seed and implements, and B doing the work, B taking one-half of the crop. Is it a partnership?
3. A and B are partners in the grocery business. A buys a horse and gives a note in the firm name in payment. Discuss the obligation of the firm to pay the note.
4. After a partnership is dissolved, one of the partners orders a bill of goods in the firm name. Can the firm be compelled to pay for the goods?

5. A and B are engaged in the real estate business as partners. A buys a piece of property, and immediately resells
it at a profit. He does not pay for the land until he is
paid. Must he account to B for a share of the profits?

6. A and B are partners in a grocery business. A wishes to
buy a large amount of flour. B objects and the flour is not
bought. It turns out that had the flour been purchased,
a large profit would have been realized. Is B liable to A
for the loss? Would such conduct on B's part justify A
in applying for a Decree of Dissolution?

CHAPTER XXX.

CORPORATIONS.

DEFINITION.—A corporation is a creature of the law having certain powers and duties of a natural person.

Being created by law, a corporation has only such powers as may be specially granted it by the law, or which are necessarily implied, and required in order to carry out such powers as are expressly given.

They are divided into two classes:

(1) Sole; and

(2) Aggregate.

CORPORATIONS SOLE.—These corporations are quite common in England and some other European countries, but are little known in America.

As the name indicates, they consist of one person in whom is invested an artificial being with prescribed powers and duties.

In England the sovereign is a corporation sole; also bishops and other high officials in the established church. The principal object in creating these certain officials corporations is that they may have the power of succession; that is to say, when the individual dies, the corporation lives, and thus the new bishop or church officer takes the place of the other as such official, without any formal changing of title, or probating of the estate.

So it is when the sovereign dies, the next in succession is, by virtue of law, considered king the instant life has departed from the sovereign.

These corporations concern us, however, but little, except as a matter of history.

(180)

CORPORATIONS AGGREGATE, as the name indicates, are composed of a number of persons, usually associated together for the transaction of business.

CHARITABLE CORPORATIONS are such corporations aggregate as are formed for assisting the indigent, or for educational purposes, and also what are sometimes called religious corporations, those formed for the purpose of caring for the property of churches and societies of like nature, are included under the head of charitable corporations.

CIVIL CORPORATIONS include all other corporations aggregate, and are further divided into two classes,—public and private.

PUBLIC CORPORATIONS are those which are formed for governmental purposes,—counties, cities, towns, school districts, and townships, are common examples of public corporations.

After a city has been incorporated it has power to enact for its own government such laws as do not conflict with the general laws.

Hence, such a city may levy taxes within its boundaries for the improvement of streets, the building of sewer systems, or supplying the city with water, or any such like purpose.

It may also regulate the sale of foods or drinks, so far as such regulations do not conflict with State or National laws.

They may sue and be sued in their corporate name. All this, it will be readily seen, is of great advantage to any community.

Such corporations are formed by charter from the State Legislature, or under general laws.

These general laws must be strictly followed in order properly to form the public corporation.

PRIVATE CORPORATIONS.—It is this class of corporations which we wish particularly to consider in our discussion of the subject.

The business of private corporations comprises every line of commercial enterprise, and the formation of such corporations affords a means of combining individual wealth so that gigantic enterprises are undertaken and carried through, which would otherwise be impossible or extremely difficult.

Nearly all railroad, canal, steamboat, and other companies, doing a large business, are incorporated.

Private corporations may be formed for any purpose for which individuals may lawfully associate themselves.

FORMATION.—Private corporations may be formed by the voluntary association of any five or more persons, a majority of such persons being residents of the State in which the corporation is formed.

Such formation is under general statute. Formation by charter is superseded so far as private corporations are concerned.

ARTICLES OF INCORPORATION.—The instrument by which a private corporation is formed, is called "Articles of Incorporation." Such Articles must be prepared setting forth,

(1) The name of the incorporation;

(2) Its purpose;

(3) The place where its principal business is to be transacted;

(4) The term of existence, not exceeding fifty years;

(5) The number of its directors; not less than five nor more than eleven;

(6) The amount of its capital stock, and the number of shares thereof;

(7) The amount of capital stock subscribed, and by whom.

These Articles are filed with the County Clerk of the county in which the principal business of the company is to be transacted, and a certified copy filed with the Secretary of State, who, upon such filing, must issue to the corporation, under seal of the State, a certificate to the effect that such Articles are filed.

When these proceedings are had, the company may then proceed to make by-laws, elect officers, and transact business generally, as provided for in their Articles.

Sometimes no capital stock is issued. In such case, of course, this fact must be stated in the Articles.

AGREEMENTS FOR STOCK.—When an undertaking of great magnitude is begun, such as the building of a railroad, it is usual for those who first enter into the enterprise, and who are called "promoters," to circulate a paper called a subscription paper, headed something like this:

"January 2d, 1897.

"We, the undersigned, hereby subscribe for, and agree to purchase the number of shares of stock set opposite our respective names at a price of $10 per share, at any time within One (1) year from date hereof" (or, "when the total amount of 10,000 shares are subscribed," or any other like condition).

Such stock subscriptions are binding upon the signers, the consideration being the detriment caused to the promoters and the co-signers by reason of the withholding of money from other purposes for stock payments.

However, in case of conditional agreements like the above, the subscription does not become absolutely binding until the condition is fulfilled.

CERTIFICATE OF STOCK.—Stock consists of the money or property contributed in the formation of the corporation, and because of many people having interests in this capital stock, the stock is said to be divided into shares represented by what is called a "Certificate of Stock."

These Certificates of Stock are mere pieces of paper issued to each stockholder for the purpose of certifying to the number of shares which he holds.

The ordinary form of a stock certificate is as follows:

Stockton, Cal., Jan. 2d, 1897.

No. 24.
10 Shares.   CAPITAL STOCK, $20,000.00

THIS CERTIFIES That Edward Johnson is entitled to Ten

(10) shares of the capital stock of THE CALIFORNIA HARD-WARE COMPANY; transferable on the books of the Company only by endorsement hereon and surrender of this Certificate, subject to the By-laws of this corporation.

R. BOYD, Secretary.

S. MAXIN, President.

✢✢✢✢✢✢✢✢✢✢✢
✢ CORPORATE SEAL. ✢
✢✢✢✢✢✢✢✢✢✢✢

2000 shares, $10 each.

To this Certificate is attached a "stub" which remains in the Certificate book. The "stub" contains the number of the Certificate, number of shares, date, name of person to whom it was issued, etc., as a matter of memorandum for the Secretary.

This stock certificate, as has been intimated, is not the stock itself, but simply the evidence of ownership of stock; hence it can be changed or divided into any number of certificates of less number of shares, not greater in the aggregate than the number of shares it certifies to.

TRANSFER.—A certificate of stock may pass from hand to hand by endorsement in a manner similar to the transfer of negotiable paper, though no holder of it can acquire any rights as against the corporation until he presents the certificate to the Secretary, and has it transferred to him on the books of the corporation.

Suppose Mr. Johnson, holder of ten shares as shown in the form above, wishes to sell five shares of his stock to Andrew White. He makes an endorsement upon the back of the certificate in something like the following form:

"I hereby sell, assign, and transfer to Andrew White, Five (5) shares of the capital stock of THE CALIFORNIA HARDWARE COMPANY, represented by the within certificate, and hereby appoint R. Boyd my attorney to transfer the said stock on the books of said corporation.

"Dated January 27th, 1898.

"(Signed) Edward Johnson."

Andrew White then takes the certificate to the Secretary, who cancels it and issues a certificate of five shares to White, and another certificate of five shares to Johnson, making proper entries on his own books.

CORPORATE RESIDENCE.—As we have seen the Articles of Incorporation are required to set forth the place where the principal business of the corporation is to be carried on, and it also requires that a majority of the incorporators shall be residents of the State in which the corporation is formed.

The reason for this is, to fix the place where the corporation may sue and be sued, and to determine under what law it shall be governed.

In case of railroad companies and other such corporations transacting business in a number of different States and territories, it is often important to know in case of conflict of laws, under what law the corporation must do business.

As a general rule the law of the place where the corporation has its principal place of business governs it in the conduct of its affairs, and other States recognize the rights which accrue to it under the laws of its place of residence.

In case of foreign corporations having general agencies in this State, the law of the State will control as to the manner of transacting their business. A common example is that of fire and life insurance companies.

POWERS.—Every corporation has such power to act in the business world as is expressly given it, or is necessarily implied for the carrying out of the express powers, and no other or greater powers.

Thus, if a corporation is given power to buy and sell real estate, there is also necessarily implied the power to execute deeds of real estate.

The following are the general powers given to corporations:

(1) Of succession;

(2) To sue and be sued;

(3) To make and use a common seal;

(4) To buy and sell property;

(5) To appoint officers and allow them compensation;

(6) To make by-laws;

(7) To admit stockholders or members;

(8) Generally, to enter into any obligations or contracts essential to the transaction of its ordinary affairs, or for the purposes of the corporation.

PERPETUAL SUCCESSION.—The word "perpetual" does not mean that the corporation may never at any time be dissolved or cease to exist by lapse of time.

It means simply that when a member dies, his representatives at once succeed to his interest in the corporation, and the corporation continues to do business without any dissolution or accounting.

This is one great advantage a corporation has over a partnership. It will be remembered that when a partner dies, the partnership is dissolved thereby.

The life of a corporation, however, is fixed at fifty years, consequently there is no power of succession for a longer period than fifty years. The company may, however, reincorporate at the end of such period.

TO SUE AND BE SUED.—A corporation may be sued in any court, and in any State where it does business; and it may also sue in any State, provided it has properly filed its Articles of Incorporation, according to the law of that State.

TO BUY AND SELL PROPERTY.—Every corporation has power to purchase, hold, and convey such real and personal estate as the purposes of the corporation may require; and this law is to be construed, as regards the amount of property, to be only so much property as is reasonably necessary for the transaction of its business, and no more.

The object of this restriction is to prevent, so far as possible, the accumulation of immense landed estates by rich corporations to the detriment of individual owners.

It sometimes happens, as in the case of a bank loaning money, with real estate as security, that the corporation is obliged to buy a great deal more property than is actually necessary for the conduct of its business. In such cases the rule is that the corporation must dispose of such property with reasonable despatch.

Under the words "hold real estate" it has been decided that a corporation may hold lands as trustee, and such is frequently done.

TO APPOINT OFFICERS.—The officers of a corporation generally consist of a board of directors, with a President, Secretary, and Treasurer, and often a managing agent, and such other subordinate officers as may be necessary for the particular business transacted.

Each member, or stockholder, has a right to vote in the choosing of directors, a stockholder having one vote for each share of stock he owns.

In case several officers are to be elected, a stockholder has one vote for each share multiplied by the number to be elected. This number he may vote all for one officer should he choose.

A stockholder may also delegate his right to vote by giving authority to another to vote for him. This other is called a proxy, and also the written authority which is given is called a proxy, and is simply a written statement to the effect that A authorizes B to vote A's shares of stock for him.

In corporations having no capital stock each member is entitled to one vote only.

BY-LAWS.—Every corporation has power to make by-laws which are not inconsistent with any existing law, for the management of its property, the regulation of its affairs, and for the transfer of stock.

The by-laws of a corporation, after being adopted by the corporation, become a part of the law governing the directors and other officers, and must be regarded as such.

The by-laws usually provide in detail as to the power and duties of the officers, and the conduct of the business of the corporation.

They must, in addition to being in accordance with the general law, be reasonable in their application, and otherwise proper.

STOCKHOLDERS OR MEMBERS.—Any number of members may be admitted into a corporation, and any number of stockholders, provided that the amount of stock issued does not exceed the amount provided for in the Articles of Incorporation.

Thus, if the amount of stock is 2,000 shares there may be five stockholders of four hundred shares each, or there may be two thousand stockholders holding one share each, or it may be divided in any other manner so that no more stock is issued than what is provided for.

The stock may be assessed for the purpose of raising money to pay expenses in conducting the business of the corporation.

A certain per cent of the amount of capital stock is usually reckoned on levying an assessment.

The corporation has power to sell the stock of such holders as do not pay all legal assessments or instalments due on stock, in case it is not fully paid up at the time of delivery.

A member of a corporation, which is not formed for profit, and in which he has no pecuniary interest, may be for proper cause expelled from the corporation, and even in extreme cases it has been held that he may be expelled even where he has some pecuniary interest; but a stockholder can not be expelled for any cause, so long as he is a lawful holder of stock.

GENERAL POWERS.—The powers of corporations have been greatly extended in recent years, and as above stated they may enter into any obligations necessary for the transaction of the ordinary affairs of the corporation.

Thus, they may take mortgages, or give mortgages on property, may execute or accept any commercial paper, but, as stated in the general discussion above, a corporation has no implied powers except such as are necessary to the proper exercise of the express powers herein enumerated.

And in particular, a corporation is prohibited from issuing bills, notes, or other evidences of debt for circulation as money. This, of course, does not apply to National bank notes, for National banks are incorporated under the laws of the United States, and governed by them, and, as we have stated in the first chapter of this book, where a State law is in conflict with a law of the United States, the law of the United States must control.

The statement, however, is in full force and effect so far as concerns State corporations, whether banking corporations or otherwise.

OFFICERS' DUTIES.—The Board of Directors, and other officers of a corporation, are the agents of the corporation in the transaction of its business, and as such agents can bind the corporation in every respect, and in a similar manner as in the case of partnership, and other like agencies.

It is to be noted as a peculiar fact that a corporation can only act by its agents. It is a creature of the law, "intangible and incorporeal," as an old law writer expresses it, and hence can only transact business by and through its agents.

The directors, as such agents, have full power to transact all the business of the corporation.

They are the trustees of the property of the corporation, and are liable for any breach of good faith in the transaction of the corporate business.

They are not liable, however, for damage caused by lack of good judgment, if they have acted in good faith.

The directors of a corporation are usually elected for a specified time, and can not be removed from office before that time has expired, except for misconduct in their official capacity.

Subordinate officers, such as business managers and clerks, are, of course, removable at any time by the Board of Directors, unless under special contract.

LIABILITY OF STOCKHOLDERS.—Each stockholder is individually and personally liable for such portion of the corporate debts as the amount of stock owned by him bears to the whole of the subscribed capital stock, and to no further extent.

Thus, if A owns one-quarter of the subscribed capital stock, he is liable for one-quarter the amount of any and all debts of the firm.

Thus will be noticed another great advantage from a business standpoint which a stockholder in a corporation has over a partner in a partnership, the partner being liable for the entire indebtedness no matter how small his interest may be.

In case of members of corporations having no capital stock, each member is individually and personally liable for his proportion of its debts and liabilities, and no further.

Thus, if there are ten members each one is liable for one-tenth of the indebtedness.

DIVISION OF PROFITS.—In case of gain in business, stock corporations usually divide such profits on a basis of so many dollars or cents for each share of stock subscribed.

Thus, if a dividend of $2.00 per share is declared, A, holding one hundred shares, would be entitled to $200 of the profits; B, holding fifty shares, would be entitled to $100.

Where there is no capital stock, in the absence of special agreement, there would be an equal division of all profits among the members.

DISSOLUTION.—Corporations may be dissolved,

(1) By forfeiture;

(2) By voluntary surrender of franchise;

(3) By lapse of time.

BY FORFEITURE.—There are two ways in which a corporation may forfeit its corporate rights.

(1) By non-user.

The law provides that if a corporation does not organize and commence the transaction of its business within one year from the date of its incorporation, its corporate powers cease, and this without any action upon the part of the corporation or the State.

(2) By misuser.

In case a corporation violates the provisions of its Articles of Incorporation, or in any way illegally uses its franchise, it may be dissolved by the judgment of a competent court on suit of the attorney-general of the State in an action brought for such purpose.

BY VOLUNTARY SURRENDER OF FRANCHISE.—A corporation may be dissolved by the Superior Court of the county where its principal place of business is situated, upon its voluntary application for that purpose.

Before it can be dissolved, a petition must be prepared and presented showing that at least two-thirds of the stockholders or members wish to dissolve it, and that all claims and demands against the corporation have been satisfied and discharged.

BY LAPSE OF TIME.—A corporation is dissolved by the expiration of the time limited in its Articles for its existence, and if no time be limited, it is dissolved at the expiration of fifty years from filing of the Articles of Incorporation.

POWERS AFTER DISSOLUTION.—The Board of Directors are after dissolution the trustees of the creditors and stockholders or members of the corporation dissolved, and have full power to settle the affairs of the corporation, and they must do so in all events, except in case where a corporation is dissolved under judgment of a Court, and receiver appointed by the Court for that purpose; and even in any event should the directors refuse or be incapable of acting, a court has power on proper application to appoint a receiver to attend to the affairs of the corporation.

JOINT STOCK COMPANIES are associations of persons for the transaction of business, and in many respects are like corporations.

They have, as the name indicates, a capital stock, and they are managed by a Board of Directors.

They differ from corporations mainly in the liability of their stockholders. In this respect they are like partnerships. Each member is liable for all of the debts, if any, of the company.

Joint stock companies are practically obsolete. Their place is taken by corporations proper, where the liability of stockholders and members is limited.

TEST QUESTIONS.

1. The cashier of an incorporated bank cashes a check to which the signature has been forged. Can the injured party compel the corporation to bear the loss?

2. The handling of money by the cashier of an incorporated bank is in the nature of a bailment. For what degree of care will the cashier be responsible in the handling of the corporate funds?

3. In case the directors of a corporation wilfully mismanage the business so that loss occurs, what remedies, if any, have the stockholders?

4. Five directors are to be elected. A has twenty shares. Explain how he may divide his vote for one or more of the directors to be elected.

CHAPTER XXXI.

FIRE INSURANCE.

DEFINITION.—Insurance is a contract whereby one undertakes to indemnify another against loss, damage, or liability arising from an unknown or contingent event.

The ordinary forms of insurance are Fire Insurance, Marine Insurance, Life Insurance, Health Insurance, and Accident Insurance.

INSURABLE INTEREST.—"Every interest in property or any relation thereto, or liability in respect thereof, of such a nature that a contemplated peril might directly damnify the insured, is an Insurable Interest."

The above definition is broad enough to cover almost every conceivable form of an interest in property, the only restriction being that it must be such an interest as will directly injure the insured in case of loss.

Thus, a partner may insure his partnership interest; a mortgagor may insure his interest; a mortgagee may insure his interest; also a lessee and lessor; a trustee, and a bailee, or all of such parties, may place insurance on the same property at the same time, provided the total amount of insurance so placed is not greater than the reasonable value of the property.

THE POLICY is the written instrument in which the contract of insurance is set forth. It must contain,

(1) The names of the parties;
(2) The rate of premium;
(3) The property insured;
(4) The interest of the insured in the property;

(5) The risks insured against; and

(6) The period during which the insurance is to continue.

In addition to these general items contained in the policy there are always other agreements, statements, and conditions inserted.

Most of these conditions refer to the care of the property by the insured, such as providing that he shall not store gunpowder or other inflammable material within the building; that he shall not leave the premises vacant except for short periods of time; that he shall use all reasonable means to protect the property from fire, etc.

PREMIUM.—The premium is the price paid the insurance company for the insurance. It is usually based on a certain per cent of the amount insured for, and these rates vary according to the supposed danger from fire, which of course is in some localities greater than in others, and would be greater in a wooden building than in a brick building.

Most companies provide that in case the insurance policy is canceled before the expiration of the term of its existence, they will return a proportionate part of the premium.

PROPERTY INSURED.—The property insured must be accurately described in the policy, together with the interest of the insured in the property.

The statements made by the insured as to the property insured, and his interest in it, are taken as warranties against him, and if he makes false statements, particularly in regard to the description of the property, the material of which it is made, its distance from other buildings, and in such like matters, he can not recover insurance money in case of the destruction of the property.

RISKS INSURED AGAINST.—A fire insurance policy covers all risk of loss by fire from whatever cause the fire may have originated, unless certain causes are particularly excepted.

Fires caused by lightning are sometimes excepted, but all accidental fires and fires set by incendiaries, unless set by the insured himself, are included in the insurance.

Loss or damage by water or other means used to extinguish fire is also covered by the insurance policy, even though nothing is said in regard to it in the policy.

If a material change is made in the risk, such as the building of a new room to a house, the company will not be liable in case of fire for any damage, unless they have accepted the risk as changed.

AMOUNT INSURED.—A building may be insured for $5,000, and it may be entirely destroyed by fire. If the insurance company can show, however, that the building was not actually worth $5,000, they will not be obliged to pay any more than the actual value of the building, and it is provided in most policies that the insurance company and the insured shall each appoint appraisers to appraise the loss; and also that the company may have the option of replacing the burned premises in the same condition as they were before the fire, instead of paying the amount fixed as the loss.

Of course, in the event that the building is but slightly damaged by fire, there could be no possibility of obtaining the full face of the policy, but only the proportionate amount as shown by the appraisement.

INSURANCE IN SEVERAL COMPANIES.—Where a building is a large one, and the amount of insurance asked for is consequently large, a company will sometimes refuse to insure for the full amount required, on account of the heavy loss to the company should the building be destroyed.

It is also a matter of good business policy on the part of the insured, not to insure a large building for a large sum in any one company, as the company may be irresponsible at the time of the burning, or may delay or refuse payment.

Hence, for these two reasons it is customary to divide the total amount of insurance among several companies, and in the event of fire these companies bear their pro rata of the loss,

Thus, a building is insured for $50,000; $20,000 is taken out with the A Company; $10,000 with the B Company; and $20,000 with the C Company. If the building is damaged to the extent of $10,000 the A and C Companies each must pay two-fifths or $8,000, and the B Company one-fifth or $2,000.

This method of pro-rating between the companies is usually provided for in the contracts of insurance.

PERIOD OF INSURANCE.—This is specified in each policy of insurance, and may be any length of time that the parties may agree upon.

It usually, however, runs either one or three years, and in order to fix the time exactly, it begins with 12 o'clock noon on a certain day, and expires at 12 noon on the corresponding day one or three years later.

The reason for taking an insurance for three years is that most companies give an insurance for three years at the same rate and for the same premium as if issued for two years.

REINSURANCE.—It will be observed that an insurance company which agrees to pay a loss in case of destruction by fire is damaged in case of such destruction to the extent to which it has insured the property destroyed, and hence has itself an insurable interest in the property so insured by it. Such insurance company may therefore insure in some other company in favor of itself to the extent of its own insurance on the building. This is called *reinsurance*.

A company obtaining reinsurance must, of course, pay for it, and hence loses money by the transaction.

The reasons for reinsuring may be that the company has discovered some fact concerning the property which makes it a poor risk; or the company may become financially embarrassed, and may wish to relieve itself from some of its liabilities in order to preserve its credit,

ASSIGNMENT OF POLICY.—It frequently happens that insured property is sold, mortgaged, leased, or the like, and when this is the case the insurable interest of the parties changes.

In order to avoid the necessity of canceling the policy, returning premium, and the issuing of a new policy, and the payment of a new premium, it is usually provided in the policy that it may be assigned and transferred from one person to another, with the consent of the company, indefinitely, so that in case of loss of property, the payment may be actually made to a person who holds it, after having passed through a dozen hands.

TEST QUESTIONS.

1. Suppose that A, the owner of a house, procures insurance upon it, and afterwards employs B to set fire to the house. If the fact becomes known can he collect the insurance?

2. Suppose A throws a pan of ashes containing live coals into a barrel containing inflammable materials, and which is directly against the walls of his house, and a fire is thereby started which destroys the house. Will his act in so placing the pan of coals be such an act of carelessness as will defeat his right to collect insurance?

3. A, in applying for insurance, describes his property as being a house containing brick flues, or chimneys. His statement is true, but it is also true that one flue, which is constantly used, is made of tin. A fire occurs by reason of defects in this tin flue. Will the representations made be such a material concealment of facts in this case as will relieve the insurance company from paying the loss?

CHAPTER XXXII.

MARINE INSURANCE.

DEFINITION.—Marine insurance is an insurance against risks connected with navigation to which a ship, cargo, freightage, profits, or other insurable interest may be exposed during a certain voyage or a fixed period of time.

The subject in general may be treated exactly as in case of fire insurance. The insurable interest may be of the same nature, and, as is stated in the definition, the ship or any part of its cargo may be insured.

THE RISK.—A marine insurance usually covers what are generally termed "perils of the sea," such as damage from rocks, shoals, collisions, piracy, or barratry, the latter being a violation of duty on the part of the master of the vessel, which results in injury to the cargo.

Loss by fire is also insured against, as well as incidental loss or damage caused by water or other fluid used in extinguishing the fire.

The time of insurance is a matter of agreement between the parties. It is usually either for a specified time agreed upon, or for a particular voyage, and when it is for a particular voyage the voyage must be accurately determined in the policy; and if, in such case, a deviation is made which results in damage, which would otherwise have been avoided, the insurance company will not be liable unless it is made in good faith upon reasonable grounds of necessity.

WARRANTIES.—The warranties in the case of marine insurance are of much more importance generally than in the case of fire insurance, and the law especially provides that in all cases there is an implied warranty that the ship is seaworthy.

A ship is seaworthy when reasonably fit to encounter the ordinary perils of the voyage contemplated by the parties to the policy.

Thus, it seems not only that a ship itself should be in proper condition, but that it be properly laden, provided with a competent master, a sufficient number of competent officers and seamen, and all necessary equipments, such as ballast, cables, anchors, food, water, fuel, and lights.

Such seaworthiness is in itself an insurance against the ordinary perils of the sea and damages of navigation. The insurance policy does not cover this. It is only the extraordinary perils which are insured against.

As in the case of fire insurance, fraud in the nature of concealing any facts material to the risk, will avoid the policy in so far as it may be affected thereby.

BASIS OF INSURANCE.—The policy may be what is called an "open" policy, that is, one in which the value of the thing insured is not agreed upon, but is left to be ascertained in case of loss, and in such case the value is to be based on the value at the time the insurance was effected; or it may be a "valued" policy, that is, one in which it is agreed that the value of the ship or cargo shall be fixed at a specified sum.

In such cases the rule of payment for loss is different from that of fire insurance.

The company in case of loss only pays the proportion of loss which the amount named in the policy bears to the valuation; e. g., if a cargo is valued at $20,000, and it is insured for $10,000, and the cargo is entirely destroyed or lost, the insurance company must pay $10,000, which is one-half of the valuation; but if only one-half of the cargo is destroyed, the company will only be required to pay one-half of the amount insured for, or $5,000.

When the ship and cargo are so badly damaged as to reduce the parts remaining to less than half the original value, the owner may "abandon" or relinquish to the insurance company all claim upon the thing insured, and demand insurance from the company as for a total loss.

The abandonment, however, must be neither partial nor conditional, and must be made within a reasonable time after information of the loss, and upon notice given to the insurer, either oral or in writing.

In legal effect an abandonment is equivalent to a transfer by the insured of his interest to the insurer, with all chances of recovery and indemnity.

The abandonment when once made and accepted, is irrevocable, unless it can be shown that the loss did not exceed one-half of the subject matter of the insurance.

Of course, an insured need not abandon the property unless he chooses, but the insurer must accept an abandonment in proper case unless by his contract he has declined to do so.

TEST QUESTIONS.

1. A vessel runs on the rocks and finally becomes a total loss. The owners of the cargo abandon it to the insurance company, and are paid as for a total loss. The company succeeds in saving three-fourths of the cargo, before the ship breaks up. Could either party claim the abandonment void on the ground that not more than one-half of the cargo was destroyed?

2. A ship and cargo are regularly insured and start on a voyage. Her drunken captain causes the vessel to be run upon shoals where ship and cargo are lost. Discuss the right of the insured to recover insurance money.

CHAPTER XXXIII.

LIFE AND ACCIDENT INSURANCE.

DEFINITION.— Life insurance is a contract by which one party, called the insurer, agrees to pay a sum of money to another when a certain person, called the insured, dies, or reaches a certain age.

The insured may have the policy made payable to himself, and if he reaches a certain age it is paid to him. If he dies before that time it belongs to his estate.

Generally, however, there are three parties to the insurance,— the insurer, the insured, and a third party, called the beneficiary, to whom the money is to be paid on the death of the insured.

INSURABLE INTEREST.—Every person has an insurable interest in the life and health

(1) Of himself;

(2) Of any person on whom he depends wholly or in part for education or support;

(3) Of any person under a legal obligation to him for the payment of money, or respecting property or services, of which death or illness might prevent or delay the payment; or

(4) Of any person upon whose life any estate or interest vested in him depends.

Thus, a sister, mother, brother, wife, or other relative, or any one in fact, whether a relative or not, has an insurable interest in the life of one whom he depends upon in any degree for his support or education.

So a partner may have an insurable interest in the life of his partner; a creditor in the life of his debtor; a tenant for the life of another, in that other's life.

It does not matter whether the relations of debtor and creditor, or husband and wife, or other relation continue, or whether the dependent state continues after the insurance is taken out or not, it is sufficient if the relation exists at the time of taking out the insurance.

This is, in this respect, unlike fire insurance, where it will be remembered that the interest must exist at all times during the life of the policy.

In case where a creditor takes out a policy upon the life of his debtor, and the debtor dies, he may claim the full amount of the policy, and the amount of the debt in addition; but where the debtor takes out a policy on his own life, made payable to the creditor, merely as security, the creditor must return whatever surplus there may be, if any, of the proceeds of the policy, to the estate of the debtor.

The policy of insurance may pass by transfer, will, or succession to any person, whether he has an insurable interest or not, and such person may recover upon it whatever the insured might have recovered.

APPLICATION FOR POLICY.—The law allows insurance companies great latitude in regard to the contract, and hence the various insurance companies have their own rules and regulations regarding the procuring of insurance.

In all of them, however, the applicant for insurance must answer in writing a long list of questions in regard to his personal habits, as to the use of intoxicants and tobacco, opium and other injurious poisons, and regarding the present state of his health, and whether he has had illness, and its nature; also as to the number of brothers and sisters he has, their ages and state of health, the ages of his parents, if living, and their age at their death, if dead; the ages at death of his grandparents, and many other questions which will guide the company in the issuance of a policy.

A company is not obliged to insure all applicants, but only those whose health, habits, and family records are such as render them what is called a "good risk."

Each company in addition to requiring the applicant to answer the questions, requires him to pass a physical examination by some physician designated by the company.

If the report of the physician is favorable, and the questions are satisfactorily answered, a policy will be issued.

The answers made by the insured, if he is accepted, form a part of the contract of insurance, and if he has made materially false statements, the policy may be avoided by the company.

THE POLICY.—As stated in the previous section, the law allows great latitude to the insurance companies, and they may issue policies containing about such provisions and statements as they choose, and these vary materially with different companies.

There are usually provisions to the effect that the policy will become void if a person travels to great distances from his residence without permission of the company, or removes from the temperate to the torrid or frigid zones, or otherwise exposes himself to great changes of climate.

Policies usually provide that a person must not change his occupation to a more dangerous one without consent of the company, and in cases where persons in dangerous occupations, such as miners or powder makers, are insured at all, it is only at a high rate of premium.

The premium on the policy is always to be paid in advance, and the policy usually provides, in case this is not done, that the policy shall lapse and become null and void.

In addition to these statements, the policy contains the names of the insured and the beneficiary, and the amount of premium.

KINDS OF INSURANCE.—Insurance companies have multiplied rapidly in recent years, and plans of insurance have multiplied nearly as rapidly.

What are known as "straight life" companies agree to pay a certain amount at the death of the insured on condition of payment of certain premiums.

An "endowment" insurance is a plan by which premium is to be paid for a certain number of years, and at the end of that time the face of the policy is to be paid to the insured himself.

This plan amounts to a mere investment of small sums for a certain time, to be returned with interest.

There are also various fraternal associations which provide insurance under a great variety of plans, under the general term of "the assessment system."

Such societies usually have no surplus, but depend on a large number of members paying each small assessments for the payment of their death losses.

ACCIDENT INSURANCE.—-This is a class of insurance, as the name indicates, where persons are indemnified by insurance companies in case of accident, such as the loss of an arm or hand, or the injury to an eye.

There are companies who make a special business of insuring travelers by rail, or otherwise, against accident. The policy usually contains a long list of injuries, with a corresponding list of amounts which will be paid; e. g.:

Loss of forefinger..............$200
Loss of hand.................. 300
Loss of arm.................. 400
Loss of eye................ ..... 300, etc.

providing in all cases that the aggregate shall not exceed a certain sum agreed upon in the policy.

Such policy usually provides also for a certain sum weekly in the nature of benefits while the insured is disabled by reason of the injury. The time is usually limited to a certain number of weeks.

PAYMENT OF LOSS.—The policy usually provides that in case of death, insurance money is to be paid within a certain time, upon proper proofs of death or injury being presented.

A life policy usually provides that an investigation concerning the cause of death may be made, and if it be found that the deceased was killed in a duel, or that he died by his own hand, they may refuse to pay the money.

The courts, however, have generally held that a person who commits suicide is not in his right mind, and that the beneficiary must not suffer for the act of an insane person; hence they have held that such conditions in a policy are void, except where it can be plainly shown that there was criminal intent on the part of the insured to defraud the company.

So in the case of accident policies, provisions are made that in case of negligence or wilful design to injure himself, on the part of the insured, the policy shall be void.

Ordinarily, then, the policy is payable within a limited time after the death of the insured, or his disability, and payment can be enforced by resort to the Courts, if refused.

TEST QUESTIONS.

1. A obtains insurance upon his life in favor of a child, which he states is his own, and which is depending upon him for support. At A's death it is discovered that A was not the father of the child. Can the insurance company refuse payment on that ground?

2. A son is beneficiary under a policy of insurance on his father's life, taken out while the son was dependent upon the father for support. In course of time, the father becomes dependent upon the son for support. What effect will this have upon the validity of the insurance?

3. In answering the usual questions on application for insurance, a man states that his grandfather died of pneumonia. It afterwards appears that in fact the grandfather died of smallpox. Will such a misstatement invalidate the policy?

CHAPTER XXXIV.

REAL PROPERTY.

DEFINITION.—Real property consists of land and everything that is contained on or in the land, and affixed permanently thereto.

Hence under the above definition, all minerals, oils, and water, including streams flowing through the land, are a part of the realty; so also are houses, barns, fences, and other like improvements placed in a permanent manner on or in the soil.

All trees are a part of the realty; but it is held that crops of grain are personal property.

HISTORY.—Most of the nations of Europe, including England, were at some time conquered by force of arms, and as land began to be tilled and become more valuable, it was then taken away from weaker nations and divided by the conqueror amongst his favorites. These in turn divided their holdings under some sort of rent, usually under agreement that the rentor should serve in the army when called upon; and so under this system, which came to be known as the "feudal system," the land was all owned by the king or ruler, and all others simply had rights in the property in the nature of leases.

A similar theory has been extant in the United States since the Revolutionary War, though it differs in this, that the United States Government has made actual sales of government land to purchasers, giving them full title.

As between individuals, however, a right to real property is not always an absolute ownership. These rights are called estates.

KINDS OF ESTATES.—Estates in real property, in respect to the duration of their enjoyment, are either,

(1) Perpetual estates;
(2) Estates for life;
(3) Estates for years; or
(4) Estates at will.

PERPETUAL ESTATES, sometimes called estates in fee simple, are those in which there is a full and complete ownership in the property.

A person, then, who has a perpetual estate may sell, mortgage, lease, or otherwise encumber the property; may cut wood upon it, or, in general, do any and all acts in regard to it which can be conceived of, so long as he does not injure the property of his neighbor in so doing.

The word "perpetual" does not mean that he must hold it forever, but that it is his absolutely, and he may hold it for an indefinite time.

In case of his death, the property descends to his heirs. If he leaves no heirs, and no will directing its distribution to other parties, the property reverts to the state, and is sold, and the proceeds applied to the public school fund of the state.

ESTATES FOR LIFE.—As the name indicates, an estate for life is an interest in real property, giving the use of such property during the person's life who thus holds it.

A person may have an estate for life, and at his death the property then reverts to whomever held the full ownership or perpetual estate.

In other words, a life estate is a part of a perpetual estate. The holder of a life estate may use the property in all ordinary ways, but he has no power to sell the land, or to mortgage, or even lease it, except for a period not longer than his own life.

In the case of a perpetual estate, as we have noticed, the owner may do any act, even to chopping down all timber or burning all buildings on his property if he chooses.

The holder of a life estate, however, must not cut timber, more than he needs for his use, nor burn nor destroy any buildings, or in any way injure the property.

If he does, he is said to be guilty of "waste," and is liable for all damage to the holder of the perpetual estate.

"Waste" may be even committed by negligently allowing buildings or fences to fall down for want of proper and ordinary repairs.

The holder of a life estate is not bound to make extraordinary repairs, such as building a new house. He is bound to pay all taxes during the time he holds the property.

While the life estate terminates at the moment of death of the person holding it, nevertheless his heirs are entitled to any crops which may be growing on the land as result of his labors, and may enter the land for the purpose of removing them.

ESTATES FOR YEARS.—This is a very common form of estate, and is granted under what is commonly known as a lease.

The holder of a perpetual estate, or an owner, is said to lease land to another, or give him an estate for years in it.

The holder of an estate for years has the same right to use the land as the holder of an estate for life.

There is one important difference which is to be noted between a holder of a life estate and a holder of an estate for years, and that is in regard to the crops or emblements, as they are called, which may remain at the expiration of the term.

In the case of the estate for life, the heirs of the life estate holder may claim them after his death.

This is so for the reason that he does not know the hour of his death, and could not be expected to do otherwise than provide for future crops at all times, while in the case of a tenant for years, he knows definitely when his lease will expire, and if he has crops in, and which mature after the expiration of his lease, it is his own fault, and he must suffer for it.

14

Of course, he may especially agree, under his contract for leasing, that he may be allowed to remove emblements after the expiration of his lease. A lease of farming land is limited by statute to ten years, and a lease of city lots to twenty years.

ESTATES AT WILL.—An estate at will is created when the owner of real property permits another to occupy it without any lease or agreement to pay rent, and such tenant merely takes care of the land for the owner.

It is often created simply by neglect of the owner, as where a tenant holds over after the expiration of his lease, or where a tenant takes possession without any authority whatever.

In such estates the owner may terminate the holding at any time, without notice.

REVERSIONS AND REMAINDERS.—A reversion is the residue of an estate left in the grantor or his successors, and commences where a particular estate ends; as an owner of land gives B an estate for life in the land. When B dies the land reverts to the owner. So if A has a life estate he may lease the land for a year, and at the end of the year, if A is alive, the land reverts to him.

When a future estate, other than a reversion, is dependent on a precedent estate it may be called a remainder; e. g., A, the full owner, may grant an estate for life to B, and at the same time grant to C an absolute ownership or perpetual estate, to begin after B's death. That is, A has a perpetual estate; he gives part of it to B and the remainder to C.

EASEMENTS are such burdens or rights attached to land adjoining other land, as incidents or appurtenances; as the right of way over the land of a neighbor to reach a highway, the right of using a wall as a party wall and as support for a building, a wall which is placed on the line dividing property belonging to two persons.

Other easements are: The right of pasture; the right of fishing; the right of taking game; the right of having water flow without disturbance.

These rights are obtained either by long usage, or custom, or are attached to land by statute.

It is to be noted that while the right of taking game is granted, still if an owner of land posts notices forbidding "hunting," any one who enters upon land for such purpose is liable, not for the shooting of game, but for the trespass upon the land.

STREAMS.—A person having an estate in land may use the water of a stream flowing through the land, or on its boundaries, for all purposes which he may desire, such as the watering of stock and irrigation of the land, so long as he does not use it to the injury of others, such as using all of the water in the stream, or contaminating it, with rubbish which would be carried to the land of others to their injury.

So, also, he may not change the course of the stream unless he returns it to the natural channel before it leaves his land.

In case of a stream forming a boundary, if it is a navigable stream, his title extends only to high water mark; but if the stream be not navigable, his title extends to the middle of the stream.

The reason for this difference is that the navigable waters are public property.

HIGHWAYS.—The state, county, or municipal government may designate such roads and streets as may be proper for the convenience of the public, and set them apart for public use.

All such lands so set apart are termed highways. Roads are often made along the boundaries between lands owned by different persons, each owner conveying the right of way to a certain part.

In such cases, each land-owner owns the land as before to the middle of the highway, and in case the highway is ever abandoned by the public, the full ownership reverts to him.

As the land is only given for the use of the public, the owner has the right of pasturage or of cutting trees upon it, or doing any other act in relation to it which does not affect its use as a public highway.

EMINENT DOMAIN.—The original and ultimate right to all property, real and personal, is in the state.

Under what is called Eminent Domain, the state may acquire title to private property for public use. Thus it may acquire property for road purposes, for toll bridges, or ferry purposes, for wharves, chutes, or piers, for reclamation purposes, sewerage purposes, telegraph lines, electric light lines, canals, reservoirs, dams, ditches, and various like public uses.

Before any private property can be appropriated to public use, under the right of eminent domain, a proper proceeding must be brought, showing,

(1) That the use to which it is to be applied is a use authorized by law;

(2) That the taking is necessary to such use;

(3) If already appropriated to public use, that the public use to which it is to be applied is a more necessary public use.

As in the case with highways, when such public use is abandoned, the land so taken reverts to the former owners.

In all cases where land is taken under the right of eminent domain, reasonable compensation must be given to the owner of the land so taken.

This is determined usually by appraisers, who are presumed to be disinterested parties.

TEST QUESTIONS.

1. A leases a vineyard for one year, which expires October 15th. It being an unusually "late year" all of the grapes are not fit for picking when the lease expires. May he

enter the premises and remove them after the expiration of the lease?

2. A, the owner of land bounded by a navigable stream, attempts to prohibit fishing in the stream. May he do so?

3. If a person who has an estate for years buys the perpetual estate in the same property, does that thereby terminate his estate for years?

4. A has an estate for life. May he sell his right to the estate, and to its use and occupancy until his death?

CHAPTER XXXV.

DEEDS.

DEFINITION.—A deed is a written instrument by which the title to real property is transferred from one person to another. The essentials are as follows:

(1) A sufficient writing;

(2) Proper parties,—grantor and grantee;

(3) A thing to be granted;

(4) A consideration;

(5) Execution, i. e., signing;

(6) Acknowledgment;

(7) Delivery and acceptance;

(8) Recording.

These will be considered in their regular order.

A SUFFICIENT WRITING.—In order that the deed may be a good contract, the writing should be clear and distinct, and the language free from uncertainty.

It is not necessary that there should be strict observance of the rules of grammar, as long as the intention is clear.

It may be as other contracts, either written or printed, or in any way engrossed upon an impressible substance, but it must be complete before it is delivered.

Any alterations or filling out of the blanks after delivery, will not give life to the deed, and where alteration is made before delivery, it should be noted by the officer who takes the acknowledgment.

PARTIES.—To make a valid deed there must be, of course, a competent grantor. He must own the property and have the capacity to convey it.

As we have seen under the general discussion of contracts, any person can make a deed who is not an infant, of unsound mind, or deprived of civil rights.

As to grantees, the same rules exist in regard to competency, except that a person under disability may accept gifts of land, or any conveyance which does not require action upon his part; so if there is any condition imposing duties on the grantee, he can not be compelled to perform them, if under disability.

The names of the grantor and grantee must be written in the deed. They are necessary in order to render the parties certain.

In deeds of property owned by both a husband and wife (called community property), both must sign the deed to make the conveyance valid.

In case of the separate property of either, only the one who owns it need sign the deed. It is customary, however, to require the signature of each party to all deeds of real estate sold by either husband or wife.

A deed to a fictitious person would be absolutely void.

THING GRANTED.—There can, of course, be no conveyance unless there is something to convey. The property must be sufficiently described in the deed so as to be capable of being easily identified.

A grantor should state in the deed the nature of his interest, whether it be a full ownership, or a half of a certain property, or all of it, or as the case may be.

THE CONSIDERATION must, as in other contracts, be either good or valuable. It is not absolutely necessary that a consideration be expressed in the deed, although it is proper and may save trouble to do so.

It is quite customary in real estate conveyances to place a

nominal sum in the deed as consideration, such as $5, the real consideration not being named, and it is held that where such nominal sum is stated, the parties will be allowed to prove, if necessary at any future time, what the real consideration was.

EXECUTION.—By the execution of a deed is meant the signing of the instrument by the grantor, and subsequent acknowledgment.

The grantor should sign his name in exactly the same manner as it is written in the body of the deed.

His signature need not be witnessed, although it is customary to have two witnesses who sign their names as witnesses to his signature.

Where it is impossible or inconvenient for a grantor to sign his own name, he may give a power of attorney to an agent to sign his name for him, and this power of attorney must be executed in all respects with the same formalities as the deed itself, and must be recorded before the deed is recorded, in order that the chain of title may be in order and unbroken.

ACKNOWLEDGMENT is simply stating before some properly authorized officer, by the person who executes the deed, that he has executed the deed, and that the signature is his signature, cr words to that effect.

The officer then endorses upon the deed his certificate, to the effect that the person whose name appears as a signature, acknowledged to him that he did execute the deed.

The proof or acknowledgment of a deed, or other like instrument, may be made before a County Clerk, a County Recorder, a Court Commissioner, a Notary Public, or a Justice of the Peace.

The object of acknowledgment is simply for the purpose of proving the execution.

The deed is valid as between the parties if it is not acknowledged, but it can not be recorded unless acknowledged, and hence it is not valid as against third parties having no notice of its existence. A married woman may acknowledge a deed in the same manner and with the same effect as if unmarried.

DELIVERY AND ACCEPTANCE.—These acts are absolutely essential to the validity of a deed. As long as it remains in the possession of the grantor, it is mere waste paper, and so it is if it should be stolen, and by the thief delivered to the grantee.

The grantor, or his duly authorized agent, alone may deliver the deed. The rule is the same in regard to acceptance. Only the grantee or his duly authorized agent may accept the deed.

The delivery of the deed, as in case of delivery of any personal property, may be either actual or constructive, that is, it may be actually placed in the hands of the grantee, or it may be placed under the control of the grantee, where he can readily reduce it to actual possession.

Delivery should not be made until after acknowledgment, in order that the grantee may be fully protected by being able to record the deed.

DELIVERY IN ESCROW.—A deed may be deposited by the grantor with a third person to be delivered to the grantee on the performance of a condition, and when the condition is performed and the deed delivered by the depositary, it will take effect. While in the possession of the third person and subject to the condition, it is called an escrow. The delivery to the depositary is called a delivery in escrow.

When final delivery is made by the depositary to the grantee, the deed becomes effective from the time it was delivered to the depositary.

EXAMPLE.—A person in expectation of death sometimes delivers a deed of his property in escrow, to be delivered to the grantee at his death. When he dies, and the depositary delivers the deed, the title of the grantee becomes complete from the time of the first delivery.

The form of a deed in escrow is not necessarily different from that of other deeds, but it is best to accompany the deed by a memorandum in writing, signed by the grantor, explaining the nature of the deed.

RECORDING.—The County Recorder of every county is required to keep books called record books, in which he must record or copy, word for word, and figure for figure, every instrument properly deposited with him for record.

This copying of instruments into these record books is called "recording."

The Recorder keeps separate books for separate instruments. It is his duty to record documents in the order in which they were received; so for the purpose of determining which of two documents has been first recorded, an instrument is deemed to be recorded as soon as it is placed in the Recorder's office.

It is the Recorder's duty to indorse upon each instrument offered for record, the exact time, day, hour, and minute, at which the instrument was offered.

After the contents of the instrument are properly copied in the record book, the Recorder must further endorse on the deed the number of the volume, and the page at which the record of the deed may be found.

The original deed may then be returned to the person who desires its recordation.

EFFECT OF RECORDING.—As we have seen, as between parties thereto, and to any one having knowledge of the transaction, a deed is valid after delivery is had, whether it is recorded or not, but as regards subsequent purchasers, mortgages, and persons having judgment liens against the property, an unrecorded deed is void.

It will be observed therefore that it is of the highest importance that a purchaser should record his deed immediately upon receiving it.

If he does this, the law presumes by that act that the world has notice of the transaction, and no one can claim to be ignorant of it; and any judgment rendered against the grantor after such recording, or any second sale made by him in fraud of the first one, would be absolutely void as against the rights of the grantee.

FORMS OF DEEDS.—The common law provided very lengthy and cumbersome forms for transfer of real property, and had a variety of deeds containing different warranties and conditions.

Our modern statutes have simplified these forms to a great extent. The following form is prescribed as sufficient by the Civil Code of California:—

"I, A B, grant to C D all that real property situated in San Joaquin County, State of California, bounded and described as follows: Being the West One-half of Section Two, Township One North, Range Three East, M. D. B. & M., containing Three Hundred and Twenty (320) acres of land, more or less.

"WITNESS My hand this 1st day of July, 1898.

"A B."

It will be noticed that the above form omits the recital of a consideration, as the recital of a consideration is unnecessary in any kind of a written contract. It may be proved orally.

It also omits any statement regarding a seal, seals being practically abolished.

In writing out deeds, however, many add a clause to the effect that the grantor will warrant and defend the title.

This he is bound to do, however, in any event, so that there is no longer any distinction between warranty deeds and others.

QUIT-CLAIM DEED.—This is a form of deed given for the purpose of removing a cloud upon the title, or making the record clear.

The person giving the deed may not even claim any interest, but he may at some time have had some interest which is not properly released; hence for the purpose of disclaiming any title to the property, he gives what is called a Quit-claim Deed; *e. g.*, A may have owned a small interest in certain land upon which there was a mortgage. When the mortgage was foreclosed, he was not properly served with notice of the proceedings. Ten years pass, and while he is, as a matter of law, debarred from making any claim to the land, still the record is not perfect, and in order to release his apparent claim, he will sign a quit-claim deed.

The operative part of a quit-claim deed is about as follows:

"I, A B, have remised, released, and quit-claimed, and do hereby remise, release, and quit-claim unto C D all that tract of land described as follows:" etc.

As a matter of course, a person who gives a quit-claim deed does not give any covenants or warranties in regard to the property.

TEST QUESTIONS.

1. A executes a power of attorney to B to sell land. B has the power of attorney recorded. Before B sells the land, a judgment is recorded against the land and against A. Would the purchaser take the land subject to the judgment lien, or free from it?

2. A executes a deed of certain property to B. Afterwards A executes another deed of the same property to C. Illustrate different circumstances under which either B or C might lawfully claim the ownership of the land.

3. A attempts to deliver a deed of property to B at a distance by sending the deed by mail. The deed is lost, and never reaches B. Is the delivery complete?

4. A executes a deed of certain land to B. There is a house on the land, but it is not mentioned in the deed. Will the deed pass title to the house? Discuss fully.

CHAPTER XXXVI.

MORTGAGES.

DEFINITION.—As has been before observed, under the common law system, mortgages were regarded as conditional sales. The actual title to the property passed, with a mere right of buying back.

Under our modern system this is not the case. A mortgage is defined as follows: "Mortgage is a contract by which specific property is hypothecated for the performance of an act without necessity of a change of possession."

A mortgage can be created, renewed, or extended only by a writing executed with the formalities required in the case of a grant of real property.

It will thus be seen from the definition that a mortgage is a mere lien upon property, independent of possession, the evidence of the lien being the writing.

The modern theory of mortgages, of course, does not prohibit a person from making a conditional sale of his real estate should he see fit.

PARTIES.—The parties to a mortgage are the mortgagor, the one who executes the mortgage, and the mortgagee, the one to whom it is executed.

As in other contracts, all competent persons may be parties to a mortgage.

In case of mortgage of community property, both husband and wife must sign the mortgage. In case of the separate property of either, only the one whose property is mortgaged need sign.

It is customary, however, for each to sign all mortgages made by either.

FORM OF MORTGAGE.—As in the case of a grant of real property, the common law form of mortgage was a very cumbersome one.

The following is the modern form of mortgage of real estate:

THIS MORTGAGE, Made the 1st day of July, in the year 1898, by A B, of Stockton, San Joaquin County, California, mortgagor, to C D, of the same place, mortgagee,

WITNESSETH: That the mortgagor mortgages to the mortgagee all that certain property described as being Section Four (4), Township One (1) South, Range Two (2) East, M. D. B. & M., and containing Six Hundred and Forty (640) acres of land, as security for the payment to him of Two Thousand ($2,000.00) Dollars on the 1st day of July, 1899, according to the terms of a certain promissory note, a copy of which is as follows:—
$2,000.00

Stockton, Cal., July 1st, 1898.

One year after date I promise to pay to C D, or order, Two Thousand ($2,000.00) Dollars, with interest thereon at the rate of Ten (10) per cent per annum.

A B.

IN WITNESS WHEREOF, I have hereunto set my hand this 1st day of July, 1898.

Signed and delivered in the presence of

. . . .
. . . .

A B.

Besides the above, there may be additional clauses to the effect that the mortgagor will pay all taxes, except what is assessed on the mortgage itself, and will keep buildings insured on mortgaged property, and assign the policy of insurance to the mortgagee.

WHAT MAY BE MORTGAGED.—Any interest in real property, which is capable of being transferred by deed, may be mortgaged.

An estate for years, or for life, can therefore be mortgaged as well as a perpetual estate.

In such cases, however, should the mortgagee foreclose, he can only get such interest in the land as his mortgagor had, and not an absolute title.

RENTS AND PROFITS.—The mortgagor, being usually in possession of the mortgaged property, is entitled to the rents and profits from the mortgaged premises until the time the mortgage is foreclosed.

After the mortgage is foreclosed, the mortgagee is entitled to the rents and profits from the date of the decree of foreclosure, and if he is in possession, he is entitled to the rents and profits of the land accruing after his entry into possession.

In cases where the land has been leased by the mortgagor, the lessee must pay the rent to the mortgagee from the time he becomes entitled to possession of the land.

ASSIGNMENT OF THE MORTGAGE.—An assignment of a mortgage may be made either by writing on the back of the mortgage itself a statement to the effect that the mortgage is assigned and transferred from the holder to another, together with the delivery of the instrument to that other, and any instrument of indebtedness which there may be, such as a promissory note; or a formal written assignment may be made by a separate instrument, and acknowledged and recorded in like manner as the original mortgage.

The following is the ordinary form of assignment:—

KNOW ALL MEN BY THESE PRESENTS, That I, A B, of Stockton, California, have granted, bargained, sold, and assigned, and by these presents do grant, bargain, sell, and assign unto C D, of the same place, a certain mortgage bearing date the 1st day of July, 1897, executed by E F to said A B to secure the payment of the sum of Eight Hundred ($800.00) Dollars, together with a promissory note therein described, and all moneys due, or to become due thereon which said mortgage was recorded in the office of the County Recorder of the County of Butte, State of California, in Book 10 of Mortgages, page 400, on the 5th day of July, 1897.

IN WITNESS WHEREOF, I have hereunto set my hand the 20th day of July, 1898.

A. B.

RELEASE OF MORTGAGE.—A recorded mortgage may be discharged by an entry on the margin of the record thereof, signed by the mortgagee, or his personal representative, or assignee, acknowledging the satisfaction of the mortgage, in the presence of the Recorder, who must certify to the acknowledgment in form substantially as follows:

"Signed and acknowledged before me this 1st day of September, in the year 1898.

"A B, County Recorder."

Or where it is inconvenient for a mortgagee personally to visit the Recorder's office, he may execute a release of the mortgage by a separate instrument, which must be acknowledged and recorded in like manner as the mortgage.

The release of mortgage thus made may be in the following form:

KNOW ALL MEN BY THESE PRESENTS, That that certain mortgage made by C D, of San Joaquin County, California, the party of the first part, to A B, of the same place, the party of the second part, and recorded in the office of the County Recorder of the County of Santa Clara, State of California, in Volume 40 of Mortgages, at page 251, on the 20th day of September, 1897, together with the debt thereby secured, is fully paid, satisfied, and discharged.

IN WITNESS WHEREOF, I have hereunto set my hand the 1st day of October, 1898.

A. B.

A partial release of mortgage may be made; that is, the release may be made so as to specify that a certain portion of the land described in the mortgage is released.

This is frequently done when a portion of the mortgage debt has been paid.

ACKNOWLEDGING AND RECORDING.—These subjects have been fully discussed under the chapter on deeds.

The execution of a mortgage is acknowledged in the same manner, and the mortgage is recorded in the same manner as in the case of a deed.

The effect of recording a mortgage is to give notice to the world that there is a lien to the extent of the mortgage debt, upon the property mortgaged.

When an assignment is recorded, its effect is to protect the purchaser of the mortgage from the possibility of the mortgagee's making a second sale of the mortgage debt.

The effect of recording a release of mortgage is to give notice that the land is freed from the lien of the mortgage.

PRIORITY OF MORTGAGES.—As has been intimated, a mortgage which is first duly acknowledged and recorded has priority over any subsequent liens or incumbrances.

It is not uncommon for two mortgages to be given with the same piece of property as security, and even a greater number may be given upon the same property.

In such cases the mortgage which is recorded first, must be paid first, and when foreclosure is had, if there is any surplus after paying the first mortgagee, the next in rank as regards time, takes his turn at the surplus, and so on in the order of time, if there is any surplus remaining, until the last mortgage is satisfied.

It makes no difference what the actual date of the several mortgages may be. The record books are conclusive, and a purchaser or mortgagee will be protected in relying upon them.

In general, then, the rule is that whatever is of record first has precedence. There is an exception, however, in the matter of taxes. Legally levied taxes, as a matter of public policy, must be paid in preference to other liens.

15

SALE OF MORTGAGED PROPERTY.—Property which is mortgaged is nevertheless the subject of conveyance by deed.

The conveyance, however, does not destroy the lien of the mortgage. The mortgage lien follows the property into whosesoever hands the property may pass as owner, and before he can have an absolute title, he must pay off the mortgage.

It is customary, however, in cases of sale of mortgaged property, for the purchaser either to pay off the mortgage, or execute a new one binding himself to pay the debt.

Where no such arrangement is made, the parties usually recite in the mortgage that "this conveyance is made subject to that certain mortgage bearing date," etc. (Describing the mortgage.)

In this manner the records are made to show the exact condition of the land as regards title.

FORECLOSURE.—In case the mortgage debt is not paid when it is due, the holder of the mortgage may commence an action in court for the enforcement of his lien against the property, and may obtain a judgment decreeing the foreclosure of the mortgage, and sale of the mortgaged property.

A commissioner is appointed by the court to sell the property, which he must do at public auction, to the highest bidder. The proceeds of the sale are first applied to the expenses thereof and costs of foreclosure, and then to the satisfaction of the mortgage debt.

If there be any surplus remaining, it must be paid to the mortgagor. If there be a deficiency, an additional judgment, called a deficiency judgment, is entered against the mortgagor personally for the amount of the deficiency, and any other property which he has (not exempt) may be sold to satisfy the deficiency.

EQUITY OF REDEMPTION.—A judgment debtor, or any one, as redemptioner, may redeem the property from the purchaser at the foreclosure sale, within twelve months after the sale, upon paying to the purchaser the amount of the purchase price, with interest at the rate of one per cent per month in addition thereto up to the time of redemption, together with any assessments or taxes which the purchaser may have paid since his purchase, and interest on such payments, if any.

After the property has been once redeemed, it may be again redeemed within sixty days, by a third party, upon his paying similar interest and costs; and within sixty days after such redemption it may be further redeemed, and so on indefinitely so long as one whole year does not elapse from the time of the first redemption, or sixty days from the time of any preceding redemption.

In case such times do elapse, however, without redemption, the purchaser is entitled to an absolute conveyance from the commissioner, called a commissioner's deed.

If the debtor redeem the property himself, the effect of the sale is terminated, and he is restored to his estate, and the person to whom the payment is made, must execute and deliver to him a certificate of redemption, which must be acknowledged and recorded.

TEST QUESTIONS.

1. A has a first and second mortgage on his property; he wishes to sell the property. May he do so?

2. A deeds property to B for $1,000 cash, subject to a mortgage of $2,000. At foreclosure sale the property brought $2,000. Does B lose his $1,000 and the land also?

3. A rents a house and lot from month to month. During his tenancy a mortgage on the property is foreclosed. He is not notified of any change of possession, and continues to pay to the original landlord for some time after the foreclosure. What remedy has the new owner for the loss of .the rents?

4. A mortgage is given to secure the payment of a promissory note; the note is fully paid. Can the mortgage lien be then enforced?

5. A note is given, secured by mortgage; the mortgage is released. Does this release cancel the debt?

CHAPTER XXXVII.

LANDLORD AND TENANT.

EXPLANATION.—Under the law of real property the landlord is the owner or one entitled to the possession of land, and the tenant is one having an estate for years in the land.

The term "estate for years," however, is rarely used in common parlance.

We speak of the tenant as a rentor or lessee of real property.

A lease is the contract entered into between the landlord and the tenant, and which prescribes the conditions of the tenancy.

Under the statute of frauds, a lease for a longer period than one year must be in writing, otherwise it can be avoided at the option of either party.

A written lease may be acknowledged and recorded in like manner as a deed or a mortgage.

It is customary in cases of written leases to have them executed in duplicate that each party may have a copy.

A lease should be signed by both parties to the agreement. As we have stated before, under the head of statute of limitations, a lease of farming lands is only valid for a period of ten years, and a lease of city lots for a period of twenty years.

The reason for these restrictions is that it is a matter of public convenience and policy that the ownership and possession of property should pass from hand to hand at reasonable intervals of time, and the above-named periods have been fixed arbitrarily as the periods proper in each case as specified.

TERM, DEFINED.—The term is the time fixed by the contract for the running of the lease, having a precise beginning and ending. but the period need not be definitely fixed by the contract if it is specified in such a manner as can be made certain; as "during A's minority." Where farming land has been rented from year to year, and the lessee remains in possession thereof after the expiration of the hiring, and the lessor accepts rent from him, the contract is presumed to be renewed on the same terms and for the same time, not to exceed a month, if the rental is payable monthly, nor in any case not to exceed one year.

In the hiring of lodging or dwelling houses for an unspecified term, it is presumed to be made for such a length of time as the party adopts for the estimation of the rent.

Thus, a hiring at a monthly rate is presumed to be for one month.

THE RENT.—When there is no usage or contract to the contrary, rents are payable at the termination of the holding, when it does not exceed one year.

If the holding is by the day, week, month, quarter, or year, rent is payable at the termination of the respective periods, as it successively becomes due.

It frequently is specified by the contract, however, that rent shall be payable in advance, and in such case it must be paid in advance.

In case no amount is specified in the contract a reasonable amount is presumed.

LANDLORD'S RIGHTS AND DUTIES.—The lessor of a building intended for occupation of human beings must, in the absence of an agreement to the contrary, put it into a condition fit for such occupation, and repair all subsequent dilapidations thereof, which render it untenantable, except such injuries to the premises as may have resulted from the ordinary negligence of the lessee.

The landlord has no right to interfere with the tenant in any way during his tenancy, unless the tenant is violating the provisions of the lease, or is committing waste upon the property, but the right is often reserved in the lease, by the landlord, that he shall be allowed to enter the premises at any time for the purpose of viewing them to satisfy himself that the conditions of the lease are being properly carried out by the tenant.

A landlord may, during the continuance of the lease, sell or mortgage the property, but the purchaser in case of sale takes the property subject to the tenant's rights, and can not arbitrarily remove him in violation of the lease.

TENANT'S RIGHTS.—A tenant is entitled to the full use of land for the purpose for which it was leased. He is bound not to commit waste, or do any act which will permanently injure the property.

He may cut wood for his own use while a tenant. At the expiration of his lease he must deliver up the property.

In case, however, there are growing crops, planted by him, which by reason of an unusually late season or other circumstance beyond human control, were not fit to remove at the expiration of the lease, he has the right of reentry at proper season for the purpose of removing such crops.

As regards repairs in lease of a dwelling house, if within a reasonable time after notice to the lessor of dilapidations which he ought to repair, he neglects to do so, the tenant may repair the same himself, where the cost of such repairs does not exceed one month's rent of the premises, and he may deduct such cost from the rent; or he may vacate the premises and be relieved from further payment of rent.

ASSIGNMENT AND SUBLETTING.—Unless the contract of leasing otherwise provides, a tenant has a right to assign his leasehold interest in the property to the full extent of his own term.

Such assignment does not relieve the tenant from liability

under the lease, unless assented to by the landlord, and the assignee accepted as a new tenant.

A tenant is said to "sublet" when he still holds possession of the premises, but rents to others a portion of them. By so doing he does not release himself from any part of his obligations under the lease.

In legal effect he becomes landlord of the part sublet, and the person who rents from him, his tenant.

FIXTURES are anything affixed to leased premises for purposes of trade, manufacture, ornament, or domestic use.

Formerly a great deal of discussion was had as to what were fixtures, it being held that anything firmly affixed to the realty became a part thereof, and could not be removed.

The law is now settled under the definition above given. Any article belonging to the classes enumerated may be removed from the premises at any time during the continuance of the tenant's term if the removal can be effected without injury to the premises, unless the thing has by the manner in which it is affixed become an integral part of the premises; though even a partition placed in a building may be removed, if its removal will not weaken the walls or leave them in a damaged condition.

Such articles as counters, show cases, shelving, and window shades are common examples of what constitutes fixtures.

EVICTION.—Where property is leased for a stated time, it is the duty of the tenant to vacate at the expiration of that time without notice.

Where, however, it is rented for an indefinite time from year to year, six months' notice is required to terminate the holding; and where it is rented for an indefinite time from month to month, a notice of not less than one month must be given, for such termination.

So where the renting is by the week, a week's notice must be given.

When these notices have been properly given, or when by the terms of the lease the tenant should deliver possession, and also where he has violated the conditions of his lease in not paying rent, the landlord may, in a summary manner, proceed to eject him.

This is done by giving a three days' notice, called a "Notice to Quit." This notice must describe the premises, state the amount of rent due, and demand possession within three days.

If such notice is not complied with, the landlord may bring suit, obtain judgment, and through the officers of the law, take forcible possession of the premises, eject the tenant, and remove his furniture and belongings from the premises.

It is no defense against eviction for the tenant to plead that the person from whom he leased is not the owner of the property, or that his title is defective.

Having recognized the landlord as a landlord, for the purpose of securing possession of the premises, he can not deny the landlord's authority, for the purpose of avoiding payment of his rent.

TEST QUESTIONS.

1. Discuss the obligation of a tenant to repair a barn which has been blown down by a strong wind.

2. A tenant cuts a doorway through a partition and hangs a door therein. May he take the door with him when leaving the premises?

3. A tenant is in possession for an indefinite period. He plants crops, but before they are matured, the owner sells the land. The new owner evicts the tenant. Who may harvest the crop?

4. In a lease of a house and lot nothing is said regarding the time of payment. What is the presumption as to payment, as to whether monthly, yearly, or in advance, or otherwise?

MAXIMS OF JURISPRUDENCE.

One must not change his purpose to the injury of another.

Any one may waive the advantage of a law intended solely for his benefit. But a law established for a public reason can not be contravened by a private agreement.

One must so use his own rights as not to infringe upon the rights of another.

He who consents to an act is not wronged by it.

Acquiescence in error takes away the right of objecting to it.

No one can take advantage of his own wrong.

He who has fraudulently dispossessed himself of a thing may be treated as if he still had possession.

He who can and does not forbid that which is done on his behalf is deemed to have bidden it.

No one should suffer by the act of another.

He who takes the benefit must bear the burden.

One who grants a thing is presumed to grant also whatever is essential to its use.

For every wrong there is a remedy.

Between those who are equally in the right, or equally in the wrong, the law does not interpose.

Between rights otherwise equal, the earliest is preferred.

No man is responsible for that which no man can control.

The law helps the vigilant, before those who sleep on their rights.

The law respects form less than substance.

That which ought to have been done is to be regarded as done, in favor of him to whom, and against him from whom, performance is due.

That which does not appear to exist is to be regarded as if it did not exist.

The law never requires impossibilities.

The law neither does nor requires idle acts.

The law disregards trifles.

Particular expressions qualify those which are general.

The greater contains the less.

Superfluity does not vitiate.

That is certain which can be made certain.

Time does not confirm a void act.

An interpretation which gives effect is preferred to one which makes void.

Interpretation must be reasonable.

Where one of two innocent persons must suffer by the act of a third, he by whose negligence it happened, must be the sufferer.

GLOSSARY.

ABANDONMENT.—In Marine Insurance, the giving up by the owner to the insurer of partly destroyed property.

ACCEPTANCE.—The act of a drawee in writing the word "accepted," or other words, across the face of a Bill of Exchange, by which he agrees to pay the bill.

ACCEPTOR.—One who accepts by writing on the face of a bill his acceptance.

ACCOMMODATION PAPER.—Negotiable paper, for which no consideration passes between the original parties; being given as an accommodation without intention of enforcing payment.

ACCORD.—An agreement to accept something less or different from what is named in a contract.

ACKNOWLEDGMENT.—The stating before a competent officer that one's own signature to a document is genuine.

ACTION is a proceeding in a Court, by which one party prosecutes another for the enforcement of his rights, or the redress or prevention of a wrong.

ACT OF GOD.—Damage which is caused by irresistible cause, such as lightning, or earthquake, is said to be caused by "Act of God."

AFFREIGHTMENT.—The hiring of a ship for the transportation of goods.

AGENCY.—Relation existing between two parties whereby one acts for the other in dealing with a third person.

AGENT.—A person who is employed to transact business for another.

ANTE-DATED.—Dated at a time earlier than the actual date.

APPRAISEMENT.—Valuation of property by persons appointed for that purpose.

APPURTENANCES.—In the law of real property, articles such as door keys, belonging to the realty.

ARBITRATION.—Settling a dispute by persons agreed upon for that purpose.

ARTICLES OF CO-PARTNERSHIP.—The written contract by which a partnership is formed.

(236)

ASSETS.—Property not exempt from execution, which may be applied to the payment of debts.

ASSIGNEE.—A person who takes charge of a bankrupt estate, for the purpose of dividing it amongst his creditors; also any one to whom an instrument is assigned.

ASSIGNMENT.—The act of transferring a bankrupt's property to an assignee; or the transferring of any property from one person to another.

ASSIGNOR.—One who assigns property.

AWARD.—The decision of arbitrators.

BAILMENT.—The delivery of personal property in trust for a specified purpose, to be returned after the purpose is accomplished.

BANKRUPT.—1. One who is unable to pay his debts in the ordinary manner.

2. A person who is declared by a competent Court to be unable to pay his debts.

BARRATRY.—Any breach of duty committed by a master of a vessel, or his officers, by which a ship or cargo is injured.

BARTER.—An exchange of goods, distinguished from sale, where goods are exchanged for money.

BENEFICIARY.—The person to whom a life insurance policy is made payable.

BILL OF EXCHANGE.—A negotiable instrument ordering the person addressed to pay a third person a definite sum of money, at a specified time.

BILL OF LADING.—A written contract by a carrier, evidencing the transaction of sending goods by him.

BLANK ENDORSEMENT.—A writing on the back of a negotiable instrument of the endorser's name only.

BOND.—1. A written instrument binding the maker to pay money, as penalty for breach of an undertaking.

2. A very formal negotiable instrument, issued by a municipality.

BOTTOMRY BOND.—An instrument in the nature of a mortgage, given on a vessel to secure a loan.

BY-BIDDER.—In auction sales, a person employed to bid to raise the price of articles to be sold, without any intention of buying.

BY-LAWS.—The rules made by a corporation for the management of its private affairs.

CAPITAL STOCK.—Whatever is contributed to a corporation as its working property.

CAVEAT EMPTOR. meaning, "Let the purchaser beware," applies to the case of a purchaser who has an opportunity to inspect an article before buying it.

CERTIFICATE OF DEPOSIT.—A certificate issued by a bank, stating that the holder has certain money deposited in the bank, payable to his order.

CERTIFICATE OF STOCK.—A paper issued by a corporation as evidence of the number of shares of the capital stock which a holder has.

CERTIFICATION.—The signature of a banker written across the face of a check, with or without other words, to indicate that the check is good, and will be paid by the bank.

CHARTER.—To hire a vessel, or part of it.

CHARTER PARTY.—The written contract by which the vessel is hired.

CHATTEL MORTGAGE.—A mortgage of personal property, by which it is held as security for the performance of some act.

CHECK.—A written order drawn upon a bank, or a banker, for the payment of money.

CIVIL CODE.—A body of laws, enacted by the Legislature, relating to civil contracts.

COMMON CARRIER.—One who undertakes for hire, and as a business, to carry passengers or freight.

COMMON LAW.—The ancient law of England, originating in mere customs.

CONDITION PRECEDENT.—An act, which must be performed by one party to a contract, before the other party need do any act.

COMPLAINT.—The written statement of a plaintiff in an action.

CONSIDERATION.—The inducement for entering into contracts.

CONSIGNOR.—A person who ships goods.

CONSIGNEE.—One to whom goods are shipped.

CONVEYANCE.—1. Carrying anything by land or water.

    2. A written instrument by which an estate in real property is transferred from one person to another.

CO-PARTNERSHIP.—An association of persons for the transaction of business, and division of losses and profits.

CORPORATION.—An artificial being having powers and duties of a natural person.

COUNTER CLAIM.—A claim set up as a defense to a suit, by which the defendant claims something from the plaintiff.

COVENANT.—Any agreement contained in a contract in regard to real property.

DAMAGES.—Compensation awarded to one person to be paid by another for injuries inflicted.

DECEDENT.—A dead person.

DECREE.—A judgment rendered by a court of equity.

DEFENSE.—A legal reason given by a defendant, tending to show that there is no cause of action against him.

DEFENDANT.—The party sued in an action.

DEMAND.—The act of asking for payment.

DEPOSIT.—A kind of bailment where goods are merely left for safe keeping.

DEPONENT.—One who makes an affidavit.

DEVIATION.—In marine insurance, a departure from the regular course of the voyage insured for, without necessity.

DEVISE.—A gift of real estate by will.

DIES NON.—(No days.) Holidays, or days when Courts do not transact business.

DISABILITY.—Legal incapacity to contract.

DISAFFIRMANCE.—The act of making void a voidable contract.

DISHONOR.—The refusal of the debtor in a negotiable instrument to pay it when due.

DIVIDEND.—1. The profits of a corporation distributed among its stockholders.

2. The proceeds of a bankrupt's estate divided among creditors.

DRAFT.—An inland bill of exchange.

DRAWEE.—One who is ordered to pay a sum of money named in a bill of exchange.

DRAWER.—The person who makes, or draws, the bill of exchange.

DURESS.—Unlawful restraint of person or property.

EASEMENT.—A privilege of using another's land, such as right of way.

EMBLEMENTS.—Growing crops of any kind.

EMINENT DOMAIN.—The right of the government to take private property for public use.

ENDORSE.—To put one's name on the back of an instrument in writing.

ENDORSEE.—The person in whose favor the endorsement is made.

ENDORSER.—The one who makes the endorsement.

EQUITY OF REDEMPTION.—The right of a mortgagor, or others, to redeem mortgaged property after foreclosure.

ESCHEAT.—The reverting of land to the state at the death of the owner without heirs or will.

ESCROW.—Any written instrument delivered to a third party to be held and delivered at some future time to the grantee or other person designated.

ESTATE.—The interest of a person in real property.

EXECUTION.—1. A writ issued to a peace officer commanding him to enforce a judgment.

2. The signing of any legal document so as to make it valid, particularly of a deed or mortgage.

FEE SIMPLE.—An absolute or perpetual estate in lands.

FIRM.—The members of a partnership collectively.

FORECLOSURE.—The proceedings in a suit to enforce the lien of a mortgage, together with the sale of the mortgaged premises.

FRANCHISE.—A special privilege conferred by the government; as, the right to build a railroad through city streets.

FRAUD.—Deceit practised upon another to his injury.

FREEHOLD.—Any estate of inheritance, or a life estate.

FREIGHT.—1. The price paid a carrier for shipping goods.

2. The goods themselves while in transit.

GENERAL AVERAGE.—A contribution by owners of a vessel and cargo on account of loss sustained by a person whose property has been sacrificed for the common safety.

GOOD WILL.—The expectation of continued public patronage of a business house.

GUARANTOR.—One who agrees to be responsible for the performance of some act by another.

GUARDIAN.—One appointed to have the care and custody of the person or property of an incompetent person.

GUEST.—A person who is received and furnished entertainment at an inn.

IDIOT.—One without reasoning powers from birth.

INCAPACITY.—Lack of legal qualifications to do business.

INCORPORATE.—To form a corporation.

INFANT.—A person under age; in case of males, under 21 years; females, under 18 years.

INJUNCTION.—A writ or order of a Court or Judge commanding a certain person to refrain from doing some act.

INSANE PERSON.—One who has lost his reason.

INSOLVENT.—A person unable to pay his debts in the usual course of business.

INSURABLE INTEREST.—That interest which a person has in property, or another's life, which, if the property is destroyed, or the person dies, would result in pecuniary loss to him.

INSURANCE.—A contract by which a person, called the insurer, agrees to indemnify another, called the insured, against loss from specified causes.

INVALID.—Not enforceable under the law.

JOINT STOCK COMPANIES.—An association of persons similar to partnership, but having capital stock, and a Board of Directors like a corporation.

JUDGMENT.—The sentence of the law given by a Court against the party who is defeated in the trial of a case.

JUDGMENT DEBTOR.—The person against whom the judgment is rendered.

JURISDICTION.—The extent, either in territory or kind of property, over which a Court has authority.

LANDLORD.—1. The keeper of an inn or hotel.

    2. One who rents lands or houses.

LAW MERCHANT.—The old English law in regard to commercial transactions.

LEASE.—The instrument by which an estate for years is given.

LEGAL TENDER.—Anything which is designated by law as lawful money for the payment of debts.

LETTER OF CREDIT.—A general letter drawn by a banker authorizing certain banks to pay to the holder any amount of money up to a limit, and draw drafts upon the bank which issues the letter for the amounts advanced.

LIEN.—The right to retain the property of another as security for the payment of a debt.

LUNATIC.—A person who has lost his reason, but has occasional lucid intervals.

MATURITY.—The time at which commercial paper becomes due.

MINOR.—A person under age. (See Infant.)

MISUSER.—Wrongful using of a franchise.

MONTH.—In the law of contracts, a calendar month.

MORTGAGE.—A written contract by which a person, called a mortgagor, creates a lien on his property to secure a debt, owed by him, to another, called the mortgagee.

16

MUNICIPAL.—Relating to a city.

MUNICIPAL LAW.—The law of any city, state or nation.

NEGOTIABLE PAPER.—Certain written instruments, which, under certain conditions, may be transferred by endorsement, and give the holder full power of collection.

NOTARY PUBLIC.—An officer invested with power to administer oaths, take acknowledgments, protest negotiable instruments, etc.

ORDINANCE.—A law passed by a city council, or board of supervisors of a county.

OUTLAWED.—A debt which remains uncollected beyond the time allowed by law for collection.

PARTNERSHIP.—An association of persons in business, under agreement to contribute capital, and divide losses and gains.

PARTY WALL.—A wall placed on the line between two adjoining estates for the purpose of supporting a building on either side.

PERILS OF THE SEA.—All dangers naturally pertaining to navigation.

PLEDGE.—A delivery of personal property, by a person called the pledgor, to secure the payment of a debt, to a person called the pledgee.

POLICY.—The contract of insurance.

POST-DATED.—Bearing a later date than that at which an instrument was actually made.

POWER OF ATTORNEY.—A written instrument by which an agent is appointed.

PREMIUM.—The price paid for insurance.

PRESUMPTION.—An inference of law, from certain facts, of the existence of other facts.

PRINCIPAL.—1. A sum of money bearing interest.

2. A person who employs an agent.

PROMISSORY NOTE.—A promissory note is an unconditional promise in writing by a person to pay a certain sum of money, generally "to bearer" or "to order" of some one named therein, at a specified time.

PROTEST.—A formal declaration in writing by a notary public, of his demand, and the refusal of'a debtor to pay the amount of a note, or bill.

PROXY.—A writing by which one authorizes another to vote in his place; used by corporations.

Also the one who represents the other.

PUFFER.—(See By-Bidder.)

RATIFICATION.—Agreeing to be bound by the terms of a voidable contract.

REAL ESTATE.—Land, or anything affixed thereto or contained therein.

RECEIPT.—A written acknowledgment of money or property received.

RECEIVER.—A person appointed by a Court to take charge of property, such as the property of a bankrupt, or of a dissolved corporation.

RELEASE.—An instrument similar in form to a deed, used to evidence the extinguishment of a debt.

REMEDY.—The legal method of enforcing rights or redressing wrongs.

RENT.—The sum paid for the use of real property.

RECISSION.—The abrogating, or making void, of contracts.

RESPONDENTIA BOND.—A bond in the nature of a mortgage, given for a loan upon the cargo of a vessel.

REMAINDER.—An estate which takes effect after another's estate is terminated.

SALVAGE.—Compensation for saving a vessel from wreck.

SET-OFF.—(See Counter Claim.)

STATUTE.—An act passed by a Legislature.

STATUTE OF FRAUDS.—A statute requiring certain contracts to be made in writing.

STATUTE OF LIMITATIONS.—A statute limiting the time within which actions can be brought upon a debt, or other demand.

SUBJECT MATTER.—The thing concerning which a contract is made.

SUBROGATION.—The substituting of one person in another's place, as substituting a new creditor.

SUIT.—An action on a claim in a Court of justice.

SURETY.—One who promises in writing to answer for the debt, default, or miscarriage of another.

SURRENDER VALUE.—The sum which an insurance company will pay for an unexpired policy.

TENANT.—One who has possession of lands of another temporarily.

TENDER.—An offer to carry out the terms of a contract.

TRUSTEE.—One who holds property for the benefit of another.

USURY.—Illegal interest.

VALUED POLICY.—An insurance policy which fixes the value of the property insured.

VENDEE.—One to whom anything is sold.

VENDOR.—The person who sells.

VOID.—Without any legal effect.

VOIDABLE.—That which may be made void at the option of one of the parties to a contract.

WAIVER.—A relinquishment of a right.

WARRANTY.—A statement, as a fact, of some material matter concerning an article offered for sale.